# BASEBALL UNDER SIEGE

# BASEBALL UNDER SIEGE

THE YANKEES, THE CARDINALS, AND A DOCTOR'S BATTLE TO INTEGRATE SPRING TRAINING

ADAM HENIG

FOREWORD BY RALPH WIMBISH JR.

CreateSpace

All rights reserved. Copyright © 2016 by Adam Henig. Unless it is used for reviewing or publicity purposes, no part of this publication may be reproduced or transmitted in any form or by any means, without permission in writing from the author.

This book was previously titled *Under One Roof*.

Cover design by Wootikom Hanroog. Portrait of Ralph Wimbish by Doan Trang. Photograph of Al Lang Stadium accessed from Wikipedia and distributed under a CC-BY 3.0 license.

For more information, visit **www.adamhenig.com**.

"A must read."
– Mike Vaccaro, *New York Post*

\*

"A powerful book."
– Phil Mushnick, *New York Post*

\*

"There should be a life-size statue of Dr. Ralph Wimbish on the streets of St. Petersburg. Dr. Wimbish was to this city what Dr. Martin Luther King was to the country. Adam Henig's terrific new book beautifully tells the whole inspirational story." – Peter Golenbock, author of *The Bronx Zoo: The Astonishing Inside Story of the 1978 World Champion New York Yankees* and *Bums: An Oral History of the Brooklyn Dodgers*

\*

"This book will need to be on every baseball historian's shelf, but also every civil rights historian's shelf and most certainly, it is a must-read for those who cherish Florida (and St. Petersburg) history."– Jon Wilson, author of *The Golden Era in St. Petersburg: Postwar Prosperity in The Sunshine City*

In memory of my mother, Lori Henig

# Foreword

If you lived in St. Petersburg, Florida, during the 1950s and 1960s, you might remember Dr. Ralph Wimbish. In fact, if you were a young African American at the time, there's a good chance you were delivered by him. He was imposing: six feet tall, broad-shouldered, with a booming voice and a neatly-trimmed mustache.

To those who knew Dr. Wimbish, he was a larger-than-life figure, a fighter of equal opportunities in health, housing, and education. He is credited for leading the integration of St. Pete's lunch counters, theaters, public restrooms, swimming areas, schools, and public hospitals. But he wasn't just a civil-rights hero or a physician. He was also a golfer, a bridge player, an actor, a husband, and my dad.

My earliest memory of him is sitting on his lap, telling me stories about World War II and Jackie Robinson. In 1960, when I was eight-years-old, my dad and I traveled to New York City to watch the World Series, where the Pittsburgh Pirates defeated my beloved New York Yankees. While we were visiting the Big Apple, my dad took me to my then favorite amusement park, Freedomland (unfortunately, it closed down four years later), and had me fitted for my first suit at Brooks Brothers. One year later, we returned for the 1961 World Series, and he brought me to a Broadway show, *Purlie Victorious*, the Jim Crow-era-based play that starred Ossie Davis and later became an award-winning musical.

Sports and history would continue to bond us. But during those days, we had to confront an unjust way of life—even when it came to sports. When he taught me how to play golf, we were forced to drive thirty-five miles south to Sarasota since St. Pete didn't have courses that allowed African Americans to play (eventually he would change that as you'll read). One Saturday night, I think it was 1964, my dad came home with Olympic gold medalist Jesse Owens. Thrilled to have him in my living room, immediately I phoned my best friend down the street. Other black celebrities, including Cab Calloway, Elston Howard, and Althea Gibson, also stayed at our home. Of course, they stayed with us because they were unable to get a room at any of the all-white local hotels.

When Adam Henig was researching his book on Alex Haley, he came across a 1961 article in *SPORT* magazine, which Haley had written about my dad and spring training. Realizing that my father deserved greater recognition, Adam was determined to write a detailed account of his accomplishments. On behalf of my sister Barbara and the rest of our family, we would like to thank Adam for telling his compelling story about the man we once lovingly called "Daddy." It would have made him smile.

Ralph Wimbish, Jr.

BASEBALL UNDER SIEGE

February 2016

I

# INTRODUCTION

Over the past sixty years, when reporters and baseball fans recount the historic 1961 spring training in St. Petersburg, Florida, the story that is most often memorialized and romanticized involves two people, neither of whom were expecting any playing time that season.

When it was announced that the retired Hall of Famer Joe DiMaggio would be back on the field (as a Yankee hitting coach) for the first time since he hung up his cleats a decade earlier, the entire spring training apparatus fell into a state of permanent nostalgia. Sporting his old uniform number five, St. Petersburg was abuzz. Spring training had returned to its glory days, but the story wasn't finished. Two weeks following

DiMaggio's arrival, he was back in the headlines, thanks to one of the most recognizable celebrities of the day.

During the peak of her career, wherever she went Marilyn Monroe was the talk of the town. And when she arrived in St. Petersburg accompanied by DiMaggio, her ex-husband —they were married for a total of 274 days in 1954—St. Pete and the sports media world went berserk. Monroe came from an unpleasant four-day stay at the Payne Whitney Psychiatric Clinic in New York City. When DiMaggio got word she was locked in a padded cell, he rescued his old flame and brought her to Florida, hoping to provide her privacy, sunshine, and an opportunity to rejuvenate.

Once word leaked of Monroe's unexpected arrival, journalists and the public had ditched the baseball diamond to steal a glimpse of the once star-studded couple. The two pretended to ignore the attention, but once the photographers snapped shots of the bathing suit-clad couple lying on the beach, they retreated to their hotel room at the Tides Hotel and Bath Club in North Reddington Beach. Despite the constant gawkers trailing them, they made the best of her visit: bicycle riding, fishing, and taking in several Yankee spring training games. Even though her stay lasted only ten days, the *Sarasota Herald-Tribune*declared her—not Mickey Mantle, Roger Maris, or even DiMaggio himself—as the "Yanks Top Attraction" that spring. Baseball fans and the media couldn't have agreed more.

For over half a century, the brief revival of DiMaggio and Monroe's relationship is most often referenced from that unforgettable 1961 spring training season. In retrospect, however, the story that had the greatest impact on the game and the country had nothing to do with DiMaggio, Monroe, or the Yankees. It was about a little known black doctor from St. Petersburg who wanted to eradicate the racist rituals of his hometown, even if it meant upending the traditions of America's national pastime. This book tells that part of the spring training story—a story that has gone unnoticed far too long.

# 2

# THE ORANGE STATION WAGON

March 1961

Dr. Ralph Wimbish's home was one of the nicest and largest in the Southside neighborhood of St. Petersburg, Florida. The pink seven-room home, with its manicured lawn, had a polished look and was built on a lot big enough to fit two houses. It also boasted an uncommon luxury for households in 1961: a swimming pool.

Impressive by itself, the doctor's house stood out even more in contrast to those belonging to his neighbors, all of whom, like him, were African American. Their houses were far more modest and not as well maintained. Life in St. Petersburg, similar to much of the South, was dictated by the laws of segregation. Well-to-do families of color, such as Wimbish's, had limited choices of where they could live. Even though Wimbish was a distinguished family physician and could have afforded to do so, he did not have the option to move to the upscale neighborhoods where his white colleagues resided.

In March 1961, Dr. Wimbish was expecting a visit from Alex Haley, the future author of the monumental best-seller *Roots*. Beginning to make a name for himself, the forty-year-old Greenwich Village-based journalist was one of the few African Americans in the US writing for "mainstream"—that is, non-black—magazines. His credits included *The Atlantic*, *Christian Science Monitor*, and *Reader's Digest*. Haley wasn't there to interview the debonair six-foot tall, 212-pound, well-groomed physician for a profile puff piece. He was sent on assignment to St. Petersburg by *SPORT*, a popular monthly magazine known for its in-depth sports stories that went beyond the highlights of a game.

By 1961, thirteen of the eighteen Major League Baseball teams trained in Florida each spring. If Florida was the hub for spring training, St. Petersburg was ground zero. It was the only city that hosted two Major League Baseball teams: the New York Yankees and St. Louis Cardinals. Unlike sports reporters who were sent down south to keep fans back in the chilled northern states informed and excited about their teams and the prospects for the coming year, Haley's assignment was more complicated. That season, spring training was underway and embroiled in racial controversy.

For Haley, St. Petersburg must have seemed like a time warp. Living in the hippest and most politically progressive neighborhood in New York City, he was used to rubbing elbows with whites and blacks on a daily basis. That was not the case below the Mason-Dixon Line.

Upon arrival at the airport, Haley was picked up by an African American taxi cab driver (white drivers were not allowed to transport black passengers). Haley was driven to the Southside, and dropped off in front of a two-story home large enough to house three baseball players and the homeowner, formally known as "Mrs. Williams." The Cardinals had hired her on short notice to provide room and board for first baseman Bill White, center fielder Curt Flood, and pitcher Bob Gibson.

When Haley arrived, White met him at the bottom of the stairs.

"You fly down here hot to do a story to show what segregation's like on a ball team," White informed Haley. "There isn't any segregation on the team. The segregation is in St. Petersburg—and Florida. That's the story!" Before he returned to his upstairs room, White, a large man six feet in height, shouted a few more words at the journalist as he made his way back to the cab. "Now you saw that house," the driver said. "Well, I'm going to take you to see the Vinoy Hotel, where the white [Cardinals] players stay." "I bet you ain't got nothing much finer in New York."

Built in 1926, the Vinoy Park Hotel was less than five miles away from Mrs. Williams's house, but its short distance was misleading. For all intents and purposes, it was a world away. "That's it," the driver informed to Haley as they pulled up to the 375-room hotel. Haley may have gotten out of the cab to get a closer view of St. Petersburg's largest and most prominent hotel, but he was not allowed inside.

*The main entrance of the Vinoy Hotel*

"I've heard some suites in there that cost a hundred dollars a day, the driver shared with Haley.[1] The view, Haley noted, was stunning. Green benches and palm trees dotted the waterfront. The harbor nearby was lined with yachts, and on the "Million-Dollar Pier," hotel guests, tourists, and residents, all neatly dressed and groomed, strolled or relaxed. "Colored work in there, but that's it!" the cabbie remarked. Less than a mile away, the New York Yankees stayed at the Soreno, a seven-story, three-hundred-room, Mediterranean Revival-style hotel also built on the waterfront in the 1920s and offered the same breathtaking views.

From the Vinoy, Haley could have walked the eight-tenths of a mile south along the waterfront to Al Lang Field, where the Cardinals and Yankees played their preseason home games. The ballpark was named after the town's former mayor who died the previous year and was affectionately known as "Mr. Baseball." The Cards practiced at the ballpark, too, while the Yanks practiced at nearby Miller Huggins Field, named after the Yankees' famous manager. Haley did not make the trek by foot to the stadium. He stayed with the cab. It was smart to avoid the walk as blacks did not stroll along the waterfront unless they wanted to attract trouble.

"When you get out of the game today," the driver told Haley, "you call for me and I'll take you where you're staying. And after you eat and get ready," he went on, "I'll take you to see Dr. Wimbish."

\*\*\*

When Haley arrived at Al Lang Field, there was plenty of action outside the ballpark. There were hucksters selling memorabilia —autographed baseballs, pennants, team pins. Children, black and white, stood behind the outfield wall, hoping to catch a home run. A couple of middle-aged men faced one another in the parking lot and tossed a ball back and forth. Baseball fever was in full swing.

Haley caught a view of Bill White signing autographs for fans, but when White's teammate Stan Musial appeared, the fans abandoned White for the future Hall of Famer. Once inside the stadium, Haley watched the opposing team, the Milwaukee Braves, take batting practice. Up at bat was the Braves' Hank Aaron, an African American player who was considered "one of the most valuable pieces of property in baseball" years even before he broke Babe Ruth's all-time home run record. The Cardinals and the Braves were ready to do battle. What more could a fan want beside the sunshine, freshly cut grass, swaying palm trees, ocean breeze, and baseball? The Cardinals beat the Braves one to nothing that afternoon, but Haley was far more interested in what occurred after the game was over.

"Inside the Cardinals' clubhouse," as Haley described in his article for *SPORT*, "the showers hissed, towels snapped on bare tails without regard to their color, gags and gibes flipped about in the pungent atmosphere of fresh-watered bodies and rubbing alcohol. But the camaraderie ended at the front door." The black players, White, Flood, and Gibson, made their way to the exit and encountered autograph seekers, where they spent a few minutes fulfilling the requests for a signature, then walked across the street to an orange station wagon that was rented for them by the team. Their white teammates went over to the Vinoy, where a post-game nap or a dip at the hotel's pool was routine following the game. A few of the players who hadn't seen any action on the field might have wandered off to play a round of golf.

The men inside the orange station wagon left the waterfront and crossed the tracks for the Southside whose main thoroughfare, Haley observed, was "lined with hole-in-the-wall restaurants and dank bars." There were other businesses, too, including drug stores, medical offices, barbershops, beauty salons, a ballroom, and numerous liquor stores. Still, as the driver pointed out, there was "not even a decent restaurant for them to eat in while all the rest set and chow in the Vinoy."

The residents did not fare any better. A Canadian journalist described the Southside of St. Petersburg as "block after block, unpainted shacks and tenements, some with outdoor toilets and kitchen sinks on the back porches.... In many cases, the only drinking water [is] provided by an outdoor communal faucet, to which everyone in a row of tenements [must] trek with his pitcher."

The cabbie drove Haley to the boarding house, then later, to the home of Dr. Wimbish.

# 3

# BECOMING DR. WIMBISH

During Haley's interview, Dr. Wimbish, who like many men of his era, smoked cigarettes (Salem was his preference). He explained that his approach to combatting institutional racism was through covert means, self-control, and when necessary, using his own wealth. Haley left convinced that everything he had heard about the man was true. Wimbish was indeed a "towering" figure in the black community with an "authoritative voice" and an indisputable instinct for leadership.

His home was a focal point for African Americans, especially traveling black celebrities who were banned from staying in the local hotels. Wimbish and his family boarded or hosted musicians Cab Calloway and Dizzy Gillespie, Olympic gold medalist Jesse Owens, and tennis legend Althea Gibson. During spring training, New York Yankees catcher Elston Howard stayed with the Wimbishes too. Even if they did not sleep there, ball players such as White, Flood, and Gibson came by to use the swimming pool, play table tennis, and relax since there were few alternatives available to them. What the athletes mostly came for, though, was the food. Wimbish's wife, Bette, recalled years later how she was "constantly cooking and serving" gumbo and occasionally chitterlings for their celebrated guests. It did not matter how expensive it got during spring training. Wimbish was more than willing to cover it. Their home was known as the "Wimbish Hotel."

After returning to New York, Haley submitted his article to *SPORT*, which published it in July 1961. He did not follow-up on the Wimbish story. If he had, undoubtedly he would have been impressed with how far Wimbish had come from his modest roots.

\*\*\*

Born on July 24, 1922, in Cordele, Georgia, Ralph Melvin Wimbish was born to Luther and Inez Wimbish. The couple was not married when their first son was born, and once they did take their vows, it did not last. Cordele was a small yet robust industrialized city, complete with railroad and road access, water and sewage lines, and electricity, but jobs for African Americans, beyond sharecropping and domestic work, were unavailable. Coupled with limited educational opportunities, poverty was ubiquitous in the black community. It was a period when white vigilantism ran rampant, and

Cordele in particular had a "special reputation for midnight kidnappings and mob violence."

At the onset of World War I, hundreds of thousands of African Americans left Georgia and other Southern states for more hospitable regions. In the North, factories needed low-skilled, cheap labor, but there were closer refuges for people of color. Florida, a state in the midst of an economic boom, attracted tens of thousands of blacks for its softer stance on Jim Crow and plentiful opportunities in the growing tourism industry. This vast exodus of African Americans marked the beginning of what became known as the Great Migration. Affected states, like Georgia, suffered severe labor shortages that white legislators tried to curb by instituting anti-lynching laws. These policies, however, did not dissuade blacks from leaving nor did they prevent whites from taking the law into their own hands.

In 1930, Inez, Luther, and their two sons, Ralph and Raymond, and Inez's mother, Katie McGrady Dowdell, moved 350 miles south to St. Petersburg, Florida. They lived in a modest house located in the Gas Plant district, which got its name from the "two giant fuel tanks" that towered over the area. The Gas Plant was one of the four predominately black neighborhoods in St. Petersburg. The others were Methodist Town, Pepper Town, and Twenty-Second Street South, also known as "the Deuces."

While raising Ralph and Raymond in St. Petersburg, Inez supported the family by working as an elevator operator at a downtown, white-only hotel. Luther, a barber, eventually returned to Georgia. Growing up on Third Avenue South, there was plenty for young Ralph and his family to do despite racial restrictions on their movement. They could see a movie at the Harlem Theater, eat "the best chicken in town" at the Citizen's Lunch Counter, or get a haircut at a number of barbershops. There was a variety of beauty salons, grocery stores, drycleaners, and an insurance company owned, operated, and patronized by African Americans. And there was no shortage of places of worship. Inez took her family to First Institutional Baptist Church.

As a student, Ralph Wimbish was average, if not a shade below. He attended the only black high school in the city, Gibbs High School, where he received Cs and Ds in almost every subject. Only in civics and sociology did he earn Bs, which is probably why he chose social science as his favorite subject. On his college application, under vocation, Wimbish wrote that he wanted to become a tailor. After graduating from Gibbs High School in 1940, in the fall he enrolled at Florida Agricultural and Mechanical College (Florida A&M) in Tallahassee—a historically black college and one of the few open to nonwhite students in the state. His mother and grandmother financed his higher education.

Wimbish's grades did not improve. He continued to score Cs and Ds in English, math, physics, and Spanish. In his sophomore year, his marks showed minimal improvement. Despite his subaverage performance in the classroom, Wimbish managed to find love.

Ralph Wimbish's Florida A&M yearbook photograph. Courtesy of Ralph Wimbish Jr.

Her name was Carrie Elizabeth Davis, but to friends and family she was known as Bette. She was raised across the bay in Tampa's Ybor City neighborhood, an ethnic community comprised of whites, blacks, Cubans, Italians, and Spaniards. Given its diverse makeup, it was a more tolerant population, though, it was still the South, and segregation remained firmly in place.

Like Wimbish, Bette was raised by her mother, Ola Mae, a housekeeper. Bette's father, Thomas, was an alcoholic and uninvolved in his daughter's life (Ola Mae often called him a "No good Negro"). Although Bette's mother had limited education, she pushed her daughter academically to perform at her maximum potential. Discontent with the limited options at the local black high school, Ola Mae had Bette transferred to Florida A&M's high school program, known as its "junior campus," in Tallahassee. Bette, always an avid reader, received a far superior education there than she would have back home, and when she planned for college, it made sense to stay in Tallahassee and attend A&M. Bette majored in chemistry with hopes of becoming a doctor, a far-fetched goal for a black woman given the existing racial and gender discrimination. She was also a gifted athlete, a member of the school's tennis and basketball teams. For Bette, A&M "served as a protective cocoon," and shielded her "from the racial attitudes that existed throughout southern society, while nurturing her young intellect."

In 1941, during her freshman year in college, Bette met Wimbish, a sophomore, who had just enlisted in the army and would soon leave for Arizona. He later attended Officer Candidate School in Texas, and became a second lieutenant. When he was on leave from the army, Wimbish, twenty-two, proposed to Bette, twenty, in the hallway of A&M's Charles Winter Wood Theater. She said yes, and they were married on October 12, 1944, in Wilmington, Delaware. Discharged after the war was over (Wimbish was never sent into combat), he returned to A&M.

Inez Wimbish with her son Ralph Wimbish, 1944. Courtesy of Ralph Wimbish Jr.

Wimbish went from being a mediocre student to an extraordinary one. Although he couldn't excel in psychology or physics, his grades took a dramatic turn. He scored top marks in social pathology, anatomy, bacteriology, and organic chemistry. No longer content with becoming a tailor, Wimbish selected biology and chemistry as his majors and planned a career in the medical field. Academics aside, he also caught the attention of the school's chaplain, Reverend Walter C. Wynn, who described him as a "morally clean individual" who was "honest and upright."

It was not just in the classroom where a noticeable change occurred for Wimbish. A college classmate of Bette's, Chrystelle White Stewart, still remembered seventy years later when Wimbish showed he was not afraid to question those in power. During a speech delivered by Florida A&M president William H. Gray, Jr., Stewart recalled that Gray had made "disparaging remarks" about A&M students by comparing them to those at another Florida university. There may have been a few subdued murmurs of disagreement among those in attendance, but everyone remained passive. Except for one person: Ralph M. Wimbish. He raised his hand and stood up to address Dr. Gray.

"I challenge that," Wimbish said to the college president in front of the student body. In those days, authority figures like Gray were rarely, if ever, questioned. For Wimbish to do what he did was to risk academic discipline or worse—expulsion. Neither occurred. Wimbish had stood out from his peers, determined to voice his opinion whatever the consequences. He had "instant superstar status among us premeds," according to lowerclassman LaSalle D. Leffall Jr., who would later became a surgeon and was the first African American doctor to be president of the American Cancer Society.

In 1946, Wimbish graduated from A&M and headed to medical school. Unlike his white peers, who had dozens of options, Wimbish and his fellow black students had only two viable choices: Howard University in Washington, DC, or Meharry Medical College in Nashville, Tennessee. Of the two thousand African American students who applied to Howard and Meharry, only 120 (6 percent) were accepted. Howard did not accept Wimbish's application but Meharry did.[1]

As a medical student, Wimbish was at the top of his class. Recognized for his superior academic achievement, he easily made the dean's list. Bette and their newborn daughter, Barbara, did not join Wimbish in Nashville. They lived in Tampa, where Bette taught physical education at an all-black junior high school. What she found most disturbing was the pay disparity between white and black teachers. Not only was she paid less, but she was given fewer resources, essentially "one baseball, one baseball bat, and one basketball." Refusing to accept the status quo, Bette bypassed the principal and met with the school district's superintendent. Surprisingly, he was responsive and did not retaliate, which happened frequently in the era before tenure and teacher unions. Instead, he authorized funds

---

1. Howard (established 1868) and Meharry (established 1876) were not the only medical schools opened to African Americans, but they were the only ones that were stable and provided an adequate medical education. Most of the others had come and gone, having suffered from a lack of adequate resources. Through the first half of the twentieth century, Howard and Meharry were responsible for graduating 90 percent of the black doctors in the United States.

for the purchase of new sports equipment. Bette's colleagues were impressed.

In the spring of 1950, Wimbish graduated from Meharry. For newly minted black physicians, internships were far from plentiful. Fortunately, Wimbish landed one at Harlem Hospital in New York City, specializing in internal medicine. Meanwhile, Bette searched for a home in Tampa. The pickings were slim, but she found a two-story house that was previously owned by an African American teacher. The home was large enough for her husband to set up a medical office. It was located in a predominantly white neighborhood, but since the previous owner was African American, Bette felt comfortable that her neighbors would be agreeable or, at the very least, tolerant. She signed the papers.

The day before she was scheduled to move, the house was torched and burned down. The suspected arsonist was a nearby storeowner and active member of the Ku Klux Klan. He was never charged. Distraught, Bette began looking elsewhere for her family to settle. Tampa was out, so the couple decided to start looking across the bay to Ralph's hometown of St. Petersburg.

Their problems searching for housing continued. All of the nicer homes in the cleaner and quieter neighborhoods were located in the white section of town. The Wimbishs purchased two residential lots along the "red line," an invisible divider the city used to segregate blacks from whites, and decided to build their own house. When the Wimbishs' builder went to city hall to secure building permits, he was denied. Their proposed project did not provide adequate distance from their white neighbors. A compromise was struck: the Wimbishs would purchase a third adjacent lot, and it was agreed upon that the family would not build any part of their residence on it. But Wimbish later did not let that land go to waste, so he constructed an enclosed swimming pool on the extra lot in front of the house.

The timing was ideal. Dr. Wimbish had completed his internship and was back with his family and working at Mercy Hospital, the health-care facility for blacks, and Bette was pregnant with their second child, Ralph Jr. Like most families, the Wimbishs had their routine. When the children were in school, for instance, Dr. Wimbish would come home for lunch and a short nap before going back to his office or the hospital. Even though he was obligated to heed late-night and early morning house calls on top of his already hectic schedule, Dr. Wimbish managed to spend significant amounts of time with his family.

His daughter Barbara recalled how "easy he was to talk to [and how he] didn't get upset when you had a problem." He'd often take her to the movies or out for ice cream, but if she violated the golden rule of the house—never occupy the home phone for more than ten minutes at a time so an emergency house call would not be missed—she'd be in big trouble. It was her younger brother, she recalled, who often tattled on her.

Living in a segregated city, there were only a few places outside of their community where the family could go out to eat, such as the popular Jewish deli in the Central Plaza called "Wolfie's." The Wimbishs were a happy family. Neither child could recall ever hearing their parents argue. Wimbish and his wife traveled whenever they could, flying south to the Caribbean or to Cuba before Castro took over. The children would be shuttled over to either Ola Mae's in Tampa or Inez's in St. Petersburg. When they were home, they'd often host dinners with other families. The parents played bridge as the children swam in the pool. While Bette spent her free time reading (especially books by Leon Uris) or attending women-only social functions, Wimbish made use of his spare time playing golf, going to the dog track, and performing on the family piano. To the children's annoyance, "Misty" was his favorite song, and he played it repetitively, often with a cigarette dangling from his lips.

# 4

# THE AMBASSADORS

For African American medical students, securing an education was only the first of many battles. Once out of school, black physicians had to confront the reality of practicing medicine in a racially restrictive society. African American hospitals, for example, were always understaffed. Medical equipment was either outdated or unavailable. Since black doctors were excluded from joining professional organizations like the American Medical Association (AMA), it was difficult to stay abreast of the latest research and technology within the field, and because most of their patients were destitute or barely able to pay for services, African American practitioners were forced to charge lower fees. As civil rights activist Dr. Hubert A. Eaton put it, they had to "work twice as hard to earn half the income."

Still, practicing medicine had its advantages for African Americans when compared to the other opportunities available to people of color at the time. Though black doctors were paid less than their white peers, they still earned more than almost any other African American professional with the exception of athletes and entertainers. If an African American doctor was self-employed, there was a certain level of immunity against white backlash. Other highly educated blacks, lawyers and teachers, for example, would at some point be forced to report to a white superior and consequently, had to be cognizant of their actions: personal, professional, and political.

Due to their autonomy and financial well-being, it was common for African American physicians to serve as leaders within the community. They often used their wealth and prestige to improve services for the community at large and acquire political power to try and level the playing field for their race. On the other hand, there were those doctors who were less generous and felt that paying their annual National Association for the Advancement of Colored People (NAACP) membership dues would suffice. It explained why the civil rights organization and its local branches were sometimes referred to as the "National Association for the Advancement of *Certain* People" and viewed at the time as "little more than elite social clubs that sought only to remove racial barriers that stood in the way of middle- and upper-class advancement—such as entrance to medical and law schools—and not concerned much with the plight of the black masses." In contrast, St. Petersburg had a history of African American doctors who went beyond the scope of their job.

Dr. James Ponder, born in 1888 in Jacksonville, Florida, was a World War I veteran and a graduate of Meharry. He moved to St. Petersburg in 1922, a year before the city built Mercy Hospital. Before Mercy was completed, Ponder established a two-room medical practice at a bus station where black residents, and those from surrounding communities who could afford to travel by bus, had access to care. Funded by the city of St. Petersburg, Mercy Hospital was a giant step forward for the health care of African Americans, but it would remain inferior to the city's white hospital, Mound Park.

Mercy, located in the heart of the Deuces, was smaller than Mound Park and less equipped to handle the patients it served. There were never enough beds available. Without a pharmacy, Mercy also had to rely on Mound Park for prescription drugs. To compound the racial divide, only white doctors were permitted to operate in the surgery ward at Mercy. An infant born in Mercy was ten times more likely to die than an infant born at Mound Park—a direct result of the diseases running more rampant among poverty-stricken blacks than among whites.

Over the next three decades, Ponder and three colleagues handled almost all of the medical needs of the local black population, from delivering babies to patching up gunshot wounds. Not long after Mercy opened its door, Ponder was appointed by the city of St. Petersburg as its chief of staff and remained in that position for the next twenty-five years.

By the early 1950s, however, younger doctors questioned

whether Ponder was still best suited for the job. In the opinion of Wimbish, who had begun working for Ponder at Mercy in 1951, the veteran doctor seemed less engaged with the issues of the community and more focused on pleasing his white superiors at city hall. Apparently, the elder physician embraced the wisdom of the early twentieth-century African American leader Booker T. Washington, who advised against challenging the status quo, preferring to work within the system and hoping to be offered a seat at the table. If Wimbish and his peers thought Ponder was soft when it came to race relations, Ponder believed these young men were reckless and too hasty, risking all the gains that he and his colleagues had made over the years.

Whatever threat they posed, this new crop of medical trailblazers trickled into town, most of whom arrived in the late 1940s and early 1950s, were united by conviction and sheer proximity. Their practices were located on Twenty-Second Street South, a short distance from Mercy Hospital. To those in the neighborhood, these new offices became known as "medical row." Dr. Orion Thomas Ayer, originally from Gainesville and a nephew of Dr. Ponder, was the elder of the group. Dr. Robert James Swain, a dentist and a native of St. Petersburg, was an astute businessman whose financial dealings included two hotels, one of which was aptly named the Robert James Hotel. Dr. Fred Alsup of Nashville, Tennessee, was an obstetrician. Valedictorian of his high school class and a Fisk University graduate, Alsup received his PhD from the University of Pennsylvania and his medical degree from Howard University. The last to arrive was Dr. Ralph Wimbish.

✱✱✱

"Gentlemen, let us wake up and do something to help our community," declared thirty-one-year-old Dr. Wimbish in early 1953 to a group of black, well-to-do St. Petersburg residents assembled at his home. This was the first meeting of the Ambassadors Club, founded by Wimbish to bring together the city's "*crème de la crème*, the elite, the black men who were educated, affluent, influential and committed to the community." They were the city's leaders in business, education, law, and, of course, medicine. Alsup, Ayer, Swain, and even sixty-five-year-old Ponder joined. The group helped financially and politically to support St. Petersburg's stalled civil rights movement.

The club's first challenge was the city's annual Festival of the States Day Parade. Although the parade, which was St. Petersburg's largest annual public event, attracted white and black onlookers and participants, such as the all-black Gibbs High School marching band, there were no floats that focused an African Americans. Whether it was intentional or not, the Ambassadors Club tested the waters by submitting an application for a float to parade organizers. Realizing it would be held to a higher standard, Club members put together a "first-class" float, and to their surprise, the committee in charge accepted their entry.

On April 2, 1954, a year after the club's formation, the Festival of the States Day Parade featured its first float of African Americans. Sponsored by the Ambassadors Club, the float highlighted several black teenage girls, including sixteen-year-old Rosa Holmes Hopkins who was the "queen of the float."

Although the parade might seem like a minor milestone, it was a symbolic achievement for a community who was used to being excluded. Emmanuel Stewart, husband of Crystelle (Bette's former classmate), viewed it as a matter of community pride. "We, as a group of African Americans," said Stewart, Ambassadors Club member and the black community's eminent educator, "thought we'd like to show off some of our pretty girls just like the white clubs showed off their pretty girls."

The club remained active in its quest to challenge the city's segregation policies while also serving as a social and philanthropic organization. It had established a program called Milk Fund Tea, which raised money to fund the buying of milk for the city's African American youth who could not otherwise afford it.

Prior to federally funded lunches for impoverished students, it was up to civic organizations like the Ambassadors Club to provide these services, and it did so through hosting tea parties, according to former member and retired educator Mordecai Walker. It was also a social club. After a meeting hosted by a member at his house, a group of men, including Wimbish and Walker, stayed to play poker. The doctors, Walker remembered, always gambled the most.

*Dr. Wimbish (back row, fourth from the left) at an Ambassadors Club sponsored dance in 1960. Courtesy of Ralph Wimbish Jr.*

At the club's signature events, Wimbish was usually the keynote speaker, which led to him becoming well known in the black community. A natural leader with a "booming voice," he was a quick thinker and able to respond intelligently and charismatically when pressed. No one questioned his intentions, but there were those who considered him too "radical," especially when he asked members to join a boycott or picket line. Most members were reluctant, largely because they did not have the same financial immunity Wimbish enjoyed.

Unlike his senior colleague, Dr. Ponder, Wimbish did not wait to be asked by the white establishment for a seat at the table. He sought change, though his efforts were met with mixed results. When he demanded that a segregated public golf course allow nonwhites, city officials decided to close the course and sell it to a private operator rather than open it to everyone. When members of the Ambassadors Club attended a city council meeting and proposed the construction of a youth center at a park in a predominately black neighborhood, even offering to partially fund the project, the city rejected the proposal on the grounds that the park was seldom used. Wimbish, who was present at the meeting, argued that the city had neglected the park, which explained why it was in its current state. The proposal was still turned down, but even with the failures to enact change, the political pressure the club applied demonstrated that the black community would no longer be pushed around without a fight. Matters came to a head when the club challenged the long-standing tradition of St. Petersburg's segregated beaches.

"What's the point of having separate beaches when you have a beach that your taxes are paying for?" Elwood Chisholm, a staff attorney with the NAACP Legal Defense Fund, asked black residents. "Go use it!"

Led by Wimbish and Dr. Alsup, a group of six local civil rights advocates filed suit in federal court in 1955. The judge ruled in favor of the plaintiffs. The city appealed, and the case went all the way to the United States Supreme Court. In April 1957, the Supreme Court "refused to hear the city's plea," and gave African Americans the right to use the city's beaches, but city officials, led by a racist city manager and mayor, would not abide by the decision.

On June 5, 1958, eight local black college students — nonmembers of the Ambassadors Club — purchased tickets to swim at the disputed downtown beach. After other attempts by black youths to use Spa Beach and Pool, the city closed both facilities. This created a problem. Not only did officials have "the rumblings of another Little Rock," but white residents, too, were angry since the closure occurred at the height of the summer season. In addition, the hospitality industry was opposed to the closure since it affected their guests, which discouraged tourism and ultimately hurt the bottom line. However, the city remained steadfast, and nearly seven months passed before action was taken.

On January 1, 1959, St. Petersburg's city manager, Ross Windom, resigned from his position after ten years at the helm. Five days later, the city council approved the opening of the downtown beach, and all of the city's public beaches and pools were made available to everyone soon after.

***

When Wimbish was not mobilizing the community or practicing medicine, he traveled throughout Florida, speaking mostly at churches on the topic of civil rights. He served as president of the Allied Medical Society, addressing various organizations, including the Florida State Medical, Dental, and Pharmaceutical Association, the black equivalent of the state's branch of the AMA. His stature caught the attention of the local political establishment. White and black activists asked him to run for city council, which would have made him the city's first African American candidate. To the chagrin of his supporters, he passed on the opportunity—likely due to his many other commitments.

Wimbish's increased visibility came at a cost. On May 30, 1956, four men set up a six-foot-tall cross on his front yard, doused it with kerosene, and lit it before they fled. Wimbish was away, but Bette and their two children were home. They were, fortunately, unharmed. Given Wimbish's standing in the community, the incident, which was not new to St. Petersburg, was covered in the media throughout Florida and nationally in the black press.

Regardless of the hate crimes committed against Wimbish, it was obvious that change was on the horizon. The federal government began to enforce voter intimidation laws. Liberal northerners moved to towns like St. Petersburg and refused to accept the ways of Jim Crow, and the state's newly elected governor, LeRoy Collins, wanted to modernize Florida and leave segregation in the past. Locally, the city's African American population grew from fourteen thousand in 1950 to twenty-four thousand by the end of the decade. The community had not only grown in size but wielded more political and economic clout.

In 1959, the city's buses were integrated, although African American bus drivers were still unable to obtain jobs until 1964. That same year whites and blacks in St. Petersburg were able to be on stage together and in the audience during musical performances without fear of breaking the law. African Americans were no longer forced to sit in the balcony at most local movie theaters. Even the police department experienced change with the hire of ten black officers that included a sergeant and detective. None, however, had the authority to arrest white people. In 1965, a court order overturned that policy.

*\*\*\**

With her husband in the forefront of the civil rights struggle, Bette Wimbish was not about to take a back row seat. Throughout the 1950s, while raising her two children, she was active in the community, having served as a member of the Council of Negro Women, Inc., president of Delta Sigma Theta sorority, and chairperson of the Negro division of the 1959 United Fund Campaign. She had established her own network of peers to get out the black vote at a time when people of color in the South were either turned away or faced barriers at the ballot box. Working with only a tight band of mothers, Bette "canvassed the black community" and encouraged residents to vote. She even enlisted her own children and her friends' children too. When school was out, the youngsters licked envelopes and stuffed mailers. The youth group became known as the "Hamburger Squad," since the payment was a juicy burger from the black-owned Doctor's Pharmacy at the end of each shift (The McDonald's in St. Petersburg would not serve African Americans until 1963).

Bette Wimbish, 1960. Dr. Wimbish kept this photograph on his desk at his office. Courtesy of Ralph Wimbish Jr.

As a teacher, nothing interested Bette more than the welfare of students. Like other institutions in St. Petersburg, the schools were segregated and unequal. Utilizing her background in education, Bette attended the county school board meetings and was shocked that African Americans had no representation even though the decisions made by white policymakers affected them. The board was unwilling to discuss the issues that plagued most black families, such as inadequate bus transportation, overcrowded classrooms, and below average pay for black teachers.

At one meeting, Bette learned about the district's plan to move Gibbs High School to a different location. She had hoped that the school would be transferred to a larger campus to accommodate the students better. The proposed site for Gibbs was Campbell Park, not only much smaller in square acreage (four) than the state's recommended guidelines (twenty-two), but it also served as the site of the city's largest park for African Americans. Bette learned that the board's *real* objective was to make room for a "business development." Apparently, the board was reluctant to build outside the red line. When Bette got wind of this and made her objections known, members of the board relented and found a more suitable site for their development. Gibbs High School stayed put, and a new high school, Lakewood, was built. Her victory did not go unnoticed.

James B. Sanderlin, a civil rights attorney who later became the first African American judge elected to the bench in Pinellas County, tried to convince Bette to run for a seat on the school board, following her success with the controversial high school site. At the time, Bette was pregnant with her third child, Terry. "Look, all I want to do is sit on the porch and rock my baby," Bette told Sanderlin. Perhaps, after experiencing cross-burnings on her lawn and receiving hate mail, Bette was using her pregnancy to hide her fears. Sanderlin kept up the pressure, convincing her that she had a chance to capture the seat.

In April 1960, Mrs. Ralph Wimbish became a candidate for the Pinellas County School Board. As the first African American candidate to run for elected office in the county, Bette lobbied both whites and blacks but especially whites. She delivered speeches in white parks, visited white social clubs, and shook hands with workers and patrons of white businesses in hopes of expanding voter support while demonstrating that she was a serious candidate.

As a black, pregnant female in the segregated South, it would appear Bette Wimbish hardly posed a serious challenge, yet she frightened the opposition, as evidenced by a number of death threats, topped off by a firebomb thrown at her house. Undaunted, she campaigned vigorously. She did not win, but her defeat was telling: she won an unusually large white vote, demonstrating that African Americans had the potential to be formidable candidates.

That same year, Wimbish relinquished his duties in the Ambassadors Club and took over as president of the St. Petersburg branch of the NAACP. It was a prudent move since the NAACP offered something Wimbish would never have obtained through the club he had founded: deep pockets. In addition, he had access to state-level NAACP officials and celebrities, such as Jackie Robinson, who were actively fundraising on behalf of the organization. This enabled Wimbish and his team of activists to take on their next target: James Earl Webb, a quirky, shrewd, self-taught white pharmacist.

Known to everyone as "Doc," Webb may not have had formal training in the pharmaceutical field, but his innate business sense propelled him to create a multi-million dollar enterprise known as Webb's City: The World's Most Unusual Drug Store. Webb's City was the precursor to Sam Walton's Wal-Mart. It targeted the white working class, the elderly, and African Americans. Dr. Ponder had close ties with Doc and was believed to have written the first prescription for Webb's store. Webb may have depended on his African American customers to help his bottom line, but he was a supporter of Jim Crow. Blacks who sat at a Webb's City lunch counter were either ignored or asked to leave, and it was not only at Webb's City. This was the case at almost every white-owned establishment throughout St. Petersburg and much of Florida and the South.

On February 1, 1960, four black college students in Greensboro, North Carolina, sat down at a Woolworth's lunch counter and would not leave until they were served. Before them, there were few who ever challenged the segregation of lunch counters, but the momentum of Greensboro served as a catalyst and lunch counters throughout the region were besieged with African American protesters waiting to be served. The sit-in movement was born.

A month after Greensboro, black students and residents in St. Petersburg got involved. Even Bette, still pregnant, sat down at a counter at a Jim Crow-enforced establishment and refused to leave. During the first wave of sit-ins in St. Petersburg, participants were arrested but were immediately bailed out with help from the doctors on medical row.

Dr. Alsup, in particular, was vocal about his disdain of the antiquated segregation policy at lunch counters throughout the city. "I told Doc Webb's son," Alsup said, "[when] you take down those [white only] signs [at the lunch counter], I'll start sending you my prescriptions." Webb would not budge and neither did the protesters. "What's wrong with these people?" a white lunch counter owner asked. "I have been good to you all and can't understand why you would do this to me." Wimbish and his NAACP followers held firm.

School principal Emmanuel Stewart remembered how he "was scared half to death [when he] peeped in the door" of a restaurant and found that he would be the only protester, but he stood fast for his cause. "I said, 'I'm going in there and I'm going to sit,' and they served me."

Wimbish focused his energies on the Howard Johnson hotel chain and Maas Brothers downtown department store, and successfully led the effort to integrate its restaurants. Integration efforts at Webb's City, however, had yet to make a dent. Months went by before Wimbish and his NAACP followers increased their presence.

During the 1960 holiday season, the NAACP organized a "Selective Buying" campaign against stores throughout the South, including Webb's City. "Stores that do not treat [black consumers] with human dignity or which continue to discriminate against them in some departments [will be affected]," Wimbish announced. According to a federal government report, the regional boycott effectively slowed commerce throughout Dixie.

Taken in 1960, Dr. Wimbish (center, holding a hat) is with unidentified colleagues as they board a Pan Am flight. Photograph courtesy of Ralph Wimbish Jr.

Locally, Wimbish was under pressure to back off, given the economic slowdown and complaints by St. Petersburg merchants. Wimbish stood his ground, making it abundantly clear why he would not budge. "We are not violent; we are not emotional. Some people say we should wait," he said in an interview with the *St. Petersburg Times*. "I have waited thirty years in this town and nothing has happened yet."

In December 1960, Doc had enough and sought legal action. Citing that picketing had prevented customers from entering his store, Doc secured a court injunction. The demonstrators had to leave. After the injunction took effect, twenty-two-year-old Jack Morrison was arrested for blocking the entrance to a Webb's City storefront. Although Morrison was not affiliated with the NAACP, whose members were instructed not to violate the law, Wimbish posted bail for the young man. He also tapped into the NAACP's legal defense fund to fight the injunction.

All of the other businesses that were boycotted in St. Petersburg ultimately relented, and on January 3, 1961, after nearly a year of persistent pressure, many of the lunch counters and restaurants throughout St. Petersburg "quietly desegregated." Webb's City still dragged its feet, but finally even Doc Webb capitulated.

Wimbish emerged as St. Petersburg's "most visible" African American leader. When it came to race relations in St. Petersburg, no one had made as much progress as he had in such a short period. In a memo to the NAACP executive director Roy Wilkins, Florida's NAACP field secretary Robert Saunders noted that after years of minimal turnout and low morale amongst members at the St. Petersburg branch, a positive change had taken effect "because of NAACP's new leadership." Dr. Wimbish, Saunders explained, had taken "full control" of his branch, and as a result, membership was up and meetings attracted "more than one hundred people," a number far greater than what had been seen in the past.

With President-elect John F. Kennedy about to take the oath of office and Dr. Martin Luther King, Jr. catapulting his racial justice movement forward, the timing could not have been better for the segregation walls throughout the South to be torn down. The next racial dispute in St. Petersburg went well beyond the domain of a racist city manager or stubborn drug store owner. This challenge had state, regional, and national implications. If Major League Baseball had not heard of Dr. Ralph Wimbish, it soon would. He was about to turn its world upside down.

# 5

# SPRING TRAINING IN SUNSHINE CITY

Since 1925, the New York Yankees had spent almost every February and March in St. Petersburg. A year before, the team held spring training in New Orleans, where the superstar slugger Babe Ruth was often found on Bourbon Street drinking and propositioning prostitutes (to the distress of management). St. Petersburg was an attractive (and less enticing) alternative for the Yankees.

St. Petersburg was in the midst of a building boom. Ten luxury hotels had either been built or were in the process of being constructed along the downtown waterfront. Views of the Tampa Bay, access to the beach, an abundance of palm trees, and St. Petersburg's most valued treasure, the sun (giving it the nickname of "The Sunshine City") created the ideal escape for visitors from colder climates. Led by Mayor Al Lang, the Pittsburgh-based steel magnate who moved to St. Petersburg after a health scare, the lobbying efforts to bring the Yankees to the city for spring training resulted in a major coup. It also helped that the team's famed manager, Miller Huggins, owned real estate in St. Petersburg at the time.

With the "Pinstripes" (Yankees) present, St. Petersburg had become the "unquestioned center of the spring training universe." By hosting baseball's best performing team, The Sunshine City enjoyed an incalculable benefit: national exposure. For six weeks every year, the nation's most highly circulated newspapers would run stories with St. Petersburg in its byline. Radio and (by the 1950s) television added an additional four thousand hours of airtime during the training season. On one particular Sunday during spring training, a televised Yankees game from St. Petersburg "appeared on 2,500,000 television sets in the New York area alone." What more could a tourist-centric town want?

During those precious six weeks of spring training, the city's population tripled in size. For The Sunshine City-based businesses, the New York Yankees "meant millions." As years went by, although the team's marquee player alternated from Babe Ruth, to Lou Gehrig, to Joe DiMaggio, and to Mickey Mantle, the Yankees retained its extraordinary popularity. With the addition of another club, the St. Louis Cardinals in 1938, the city became more and more dependent on baseball to fuel its economic development, but it was not just in St. Petersburg.

The spring training fever had become contagious and other cities jumped on the bandwagon. By 1956, some thirty years after the Yankees arrived in St. Petersburg, Florida played spring training host for thirteen of the sixteen teams in Major League Baseball. Nearly half the teams trained along the fifty-mile stretch of the Tampa Bay region: St. Petersburg (Yanks & Cards), Tampa (Cincinnati Reds), Clearwater (Philadelphia Phillies), Bradenton (Milwaukee Braves), and Sarasota (Chicago White Sox).

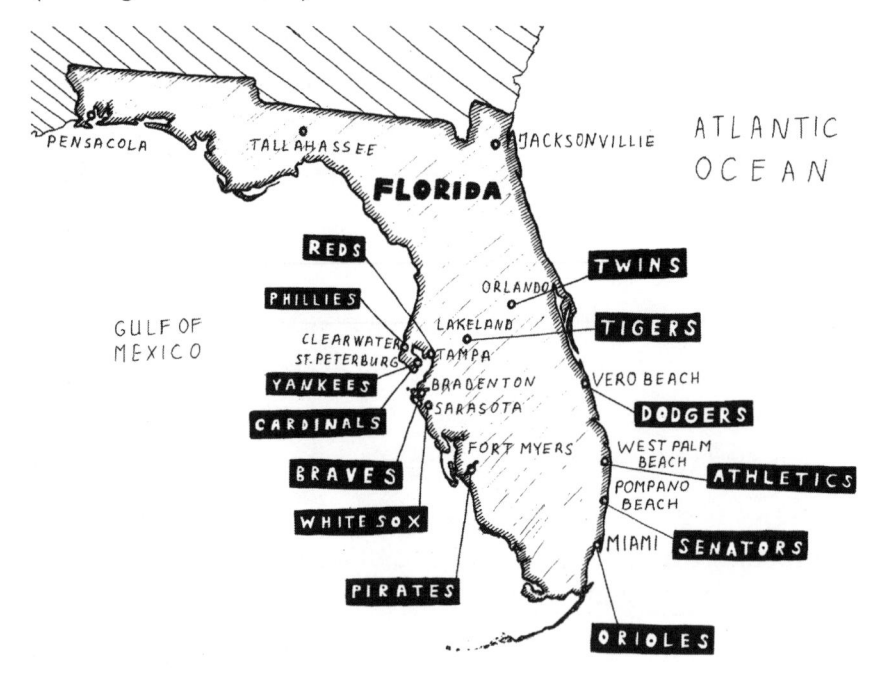

The Florida locations where spring training was held in 1961. Map designed by Darius Molotokas.

The upcoming 1961 season included several significant changes to Major League Baseball, all of which were agreed upon during the team owners' annual winter meeting in St. Louis. The owners were hoping to generate more revenue for their respective teams, so they added eight more games to each team's schedule (154 to 162). They expanded the American League by two teams (the Los Angeles Angels, owned by movie star and singer Gene Autry, and the Washington Senators, based in Washington, DC; soon after team owner Calvin Griffith moved his Senators to Minnesota and renamed them the Twins.). Baseball was moving westward.

The forthcoming season would not only reflect the decisions made in St. Louis, but the New York Yankees, the league's most successful franchise, implemented a number of changes on its own. Though the Yankees had been defeated in the previous World Series by the Pittsburgh Pirates, led by the Puerto Rican sensation Roberto Clemente, any other team in the majors that played in the World Series (and won 97 games during the regular season) would consider the season a success. For the Yankees, however, it was not. The team's co-owners, Dan Topping and Del Webb, fired their feisty, seventy-year-old manager, Casey Stengel, who had won ten American League pennants and seven World Series championships in twelve seasons with the team. Stengel was replaced by Ralph Houk, a forty-one-year-old former ballplayer and minor league coach who had never managed in the big leagues. The owners were not finished cleaning house with just Stengel though.

It was well known within the League that Stengel, a native of Missouri, used prejudicial epithets from time to time, but his boss, the Yankees' general manager George Weiss, a Connecticut native who was responsible for creating a masterful player development farm system, was a more blatant racist. In 1947, when it was rumored that the Brooklyn Dodgers were planning to elevate Jackie Robinson to the majors, Weiss told his team's lead scout: "I don't want you sneaking around down any back alleys and signing any niggers. We don't want them." Aside from his own discomfort, Weiss knew that when it came to housing its blacks players, it would prove cumbersome, during both the regular season and spring training in Florida.

Eventually, Weiss had no choice and acquiesced to the political pressure from New Yorkers, especially since the city's former teams, the Dodgers (Roy Campenella and Don Newcombe) and the Giants, (Monte Irvin and Willie Mays)— were early adopters of desegregation.[1]

In the early 1950s, the Yankees' top nonwhite prospect, Vic Pellot, better known as Vic Power, a black native of Puerto Rico, was not promoted because he did not have the "right attitude." In addition to being outspoken, it was said that Pellot had a roving eye for white women. Before the 1954 season, he was traded to the Philadelphia Athletics and went on to have a successful career as a first baseman that included winning the Gold Glove Award for seven consecutive seasons.

Weiss and the team owners were united in their belief that the first black Yankee had to have "a certain image." From the moment Elston Howard, a native of St. Louis, picked up a glove and a bat, he knew baseball was his career path and knew there was only one team he would play for—the Yankees. Howard

---

[1]. Because of management's initial ambivalence to sign black players, the Yankees missed a key opportunity to have them on their squad, which factored into the eventual downfall of their storied dynasty.

was so talented as an athlete that he was offered a baseball scholarship from a Big Ten university, but declined it in favor of playing baseball for the Negro League's marquee club (and Jackie Robinson's former team), the Kansas City Monarchs. Unlike the outspoken Pellot, Howard was shy, stably married, and had a "sweet disposition," a trait which meant he would not likely question management. In his *New York Times* best selling book, *October 1964*, Pulitzer Prize-winning author and journalist David Halberstam pointed out that Howard was "the perfect player to break the Yankees color line."

Adam Henig

*Elston Howard at Yankee Stadium, Bronx, New York. Photograph by*

*Arnie Lee, distributed under a CC-BY 2.0 license.*

Once Howard joined the team in 1955, Weiss resisted adding more African Americans to the roster. By the end of the 1950s, while many teams fielded two, three, or even four black starters, Howard remained the only African American who played regularly for the Yankees. It was rough for Howard, especially during spring training. "The camp would break at the end of the day, and you had to go back across the tracks to the black section to dress while the white boys would go back to the hotel to dress," he explained to author and baseball historian Peter Golenbock. "They would all get on the bus, but I had to jump in a cab with my uniform and go back there to dress."

By 1960, the Yanks acquired two more nonwhite players, outfielder Hector Lopez and backup catcher Jesse Gonder. Although Gonder's playing time was minimal (with Howard and Yogi Berra, the Yanks were well-staffed at the catcher position), Lopez, previously with the Kansas City Athletics, received a significant amount of playing time, taking over the third outfield spot alongside Mantle and Roger Maris. Like Howard, the Panamanian-born Lopez, who grew up enduring segregation, revealed in an interview with the author he was not the type to speak out against bigotry. "[We] did what we were supposed to do," he explained.

During spring training, Lopez recalled renting a house with Howard in St. Petersburg and rooming with him on the road. In Fort Myers, where the Pittsburgh Pirates were based, Lopez remembered how he and Howard were lodged at a funeral parlor while the team resided at a hotel. "Upstairs was where we stayed," he recalled, "and the bodies were downstairs." Fortunately, most of his teammates were supportive and did their best to make life easier for him and Howard (by bringing them food, for example, from Jim Crow restaurants).

*Before playing in the outfield for the New York Yankees, Hector Lopez played infield for the Kansas City Athletics in 1955. Photograph from "Baseball Digest," 1955, distributed under a CC-BY 2.0 license.*

A week after Stengel was fired, the Yankees' owners fired George Weiss and replaced him with the assistant general manager Roy Hamey. A veteran of the Yankees' front office, Hamey was younger and friendlier (and probably more racially tolerant) than his predecessor. The Yankees had sent a message to its players, its fans, and the media: times were changing. Even with a new coach and a new general manager, the Yankees were still the team to beat, featuring two of the best home run hitters in the game: Roger Maris and Mickey Mantle. But the most anticipated news story that spring was the return of Yankee slugger Joe DiMaggio as the team's new hitting coach at spring training. DiMaggio had been retired more than a decade and had kept his distance from the team, which did not surprise those who knew him given his disdain of the spotlight. There was a more subtle purpose to extending an invitation to the legendary Yankee. The owners were concerned that Houk, their new and inexperienced manager, would not initially command the respect that his predecessor, Stengel, enjoyed. DiMaggio was Houk's former teammate, and the connection between the new hitting coach and new manager would hopefully elevate the team's expectations.

For the other team training in St. Petersburg, the St. Louis Cardinals, who played second fiddle to the Yankees every spring, the chatter in and out of the clubhouse was whether forty-year-old Stan Musial still had another season in him. It appeared "Stan the Man" might have to hang up his cleats for the 1961 season, but the story that garnered the most attention in early 1961 was not related to Mantle, Maris, Houk, Musial, or DiMaggio. The story did not even occur on the ball field. It took place a few miles away, where very few of the Yankees or Cardinal players had ever ventured.

# 6

# "WE'RE NOT GOING TO DO THIS ANYMORE"

Wimbish had been mulling over this decision for months. Finally, in late January 1961, he said to Dr. Robert Swain, "Damn it, we're not going to do this anymore." No longer would Wimbish tolerate separate housing for African American ballplayers during spring training. No longer would he drive around his neighborhood, with a player or two in his car, seeking suitable quarters. Wimbish's routine was the same every season.

He'd get out of his car, inquire if the black homeowner was interested, and if not, drive to the next location until the players were taken care of, paying for their housing from the funds he was given by the team's traveling secretary. The affected players had been secretly informed that this practice would not continue. The African American players unanimously expressed their support, despite the risks involved. The white members of the teams had no clue.

"We told the players...we wouldn't be taking them to find housing," Swain recalled years later when interviewed by the *St. Petersburg Times*. "We said it wasn't right that they not stay with the rest of the team, and they agreed with us."

"The more I thought about it," Wimbish confided to Alex Haley during the interview in March of 1961, "the more I felt that it was wrong [and] had gone on long enough. It was high time the club and the city put them in the hotel where they rightfully belonged with the rest of the players." Though Wimbish and Swain enlisted the support of the players, could they convince those who financially benefited from the situation? "Renting to the major league teams was a lucrative business that brought up to three or four times the standard rental rates," according to Jack E. Davis, an authority on baseball's desegregation. Swain, who owned a six-unit apartment complex next to his office on Twenty-Second Street South, stood to lose $650 ($5,000 in today's dollars) a week since he couldn't charge those higher rates on the open market. "That was big, easy money in those days," the dentist remembered.

*The Swain Apartment Building once housed baseball players and other African American celebrities. The City of St. Petersburg has designated it as a local historical landmark.*

When Swain bought the empty lots to build his office and an adjacent apartment building, he was denied the building permit from the city because of its proximity to the red line. The dental office was not in violation, but the site for the apartment building happened to be located just twenty-five feet south of the segregation line. Swain threatened to sue and hired an attorney from Tampa. In July 1954, after a standoff that lasted months, the city council backed down and directed the city to issue Dr. Swain his permit. In 1956, the Swain Apartments were completed, and for the next four years, each spring, Swain rented out the units to the Cardinals and the Yankees.

Even so, Wimbish, who boarded Howard in his son's room if he was unable to locate quarters for him, and Swain agreed that they would not continue facilitating the hypocritical practice, but they were not sure if other local black landlords would take the high road. That January of 1961, while the two men waited to make their next move, columnist Wendell Smith took pre-emptive action.

\*\*\*

"I wish I could sign you, too, kid, but I can't," a Major League Baseball scout told then nineteen-year-old African American amateur pitcher Wendell Smith. Smith knew why he was not signed. It had nothing to do with his ability. He was better than the player who was signed that day. It was 1933 and Smith was black. The other player was white. From that moment, Smith internalized his anger and used it to fuel a crusade: ending segregation in professional sports. The Detroit native went to West Virginia State University, a black college, and channeled his focus on sports journalism. In 1937, the twenty-three-year-old journalist wrote for the nation's largest circulated African American newspaper, the *Pittsburgh Courier*, not wasting a moment taking on the professional sports establishments.

Within a decade of his hiring at the *Courier*, Smith had established himself as the leading black sports newsman. In 1945, the Brooklyn Dodgers' general manager, Branch Rickey, pulled Smith aside and asked him who should be the Dodgers' (and Major League Baseball's) first African American player. Jackie Robinson was Smith's recommendation. There were other black ballplayers who were as good or might have been better, but twenty-four-year-old Robinson, who had been educated at UCLA, an army officer, and recently married, was the safe choice, Smith maintained. In ways he could never have fathomed, Smith proved to be correct about Robinson —who played his first game as a Dodger in 1947.

Smith continued his journey to expose the racial inequities of baseball as well as other sports that were slow to integrate. In 1948, Smith was hired by *Chicago's American* as the first African American sports reporter at a large daily newspaper. In the early 1950s, Smith bluntly called out teams, notably the Yankees, for resisting recruitment of African American players, while other teams were lauded for following in the footsteps of the Dodgers, who had added to its roster catcher Roy Campenella and pitcher Don Newcombe. By 1961, Smith was a living legend among his colleagues and the athletes he covered. At that point, his quest for full integration in baseball remained incomplete, but he was not giving up. His next target was spring training.

On January 7, 1961, Smith kicked off the New Year with a column demanding that baseball executives whose teams trained in Florida stop supporting Jim Crow. "The time has come for big league owners to rebel against hotels which bar their Negro players during spring training. A new day has arrived gentleman." Two weeks later, Smith was at it again. On January 23, in an article titled "Negro Ball Players Want Rights in the South," the columnist told the story of three unidentified black players (most likely White, Flood, and Gibson) who were not provided boarding accommodations at a recent game in the South. With no other options, the three men were forced to walk around the town, carrying food "like a bunch of vagrants." One of the players was quoted, "[It] was quite a sight, believe me—about $250,000 worth of precious baseball talent walking down the street eating bread and cold meat in the broad daylight."

Smith's column hit a nerve in the black community and, most likely, within baseball circles too, but to the frustration of Smith and the black players, neither the teams nor the host cities took action.

On January 31, Dr. Wimbish met with the *St. Petersburg Times* sports reporter Jack Ellison. Both were well-known figures locally, but it must have seemed odd to see the NAACP branch president talking with a sports reporter. Nevertheless, the two had much to discuss. At the outset, Wimbish made crystal clear the purpose of the meeting:

The New York Yankees and St. Louis Cardinals must flex their economic muscle within the city in order to stop the ongoing housing discrimination of their teams' African American players. He explained to Ellison the paradox of his position. As the leader of the local NAACP, how could he convince his members to boycott and protest the city's segregated lunch counters but ignore the segregated housing of black baseball players every spring, for which he and others had financially benefited.

"The time has come," Wimbish told Ellison. He would "no longer help visiting [black] baseball players find spring lodging." In a written statement, he discussed further the reasons for his decision:

Living conditions for the colored players in the Florida camps are not satisfactory. The Negro is not permitted the privacy of the white man. . . . He is herded into a boarding house usually some distance from the center of town. There he must answer the dinner bell and eat whatever is set on the table. He is not given an opportunity to fraternize with his white teammates.

"It's time management of the clubs takes a hand," Wimbish declared, but the team's front office personnel weren't the only ones he was holding responsible. Wimbish had also demanded that his fellow black landlords cease to partake in this iniquitous arrangement, no matter the cost. Furthermore, Wimbish made it clear that Dr. Robert Swain, the dentist on medical row, was solidly behind his announcement.

Then came the bombshell. The decision would take effect *that* spring. Rookies, pitchers, and catchers who were always the first to arrive were scheduled to report to spring training in two weeks.

\*\*\*

The next day, February 1, 1961, the *St. Petersburg Times* published the interview under the headline: "Wimbish Declines Usual Assistance: Negro Major Leaguers Face Housing Problems." The article was the lead story of the sports section and was soon picked up by the *Associated Press* (AP). Two other newsrooms, the *New York Times* and the *New York Post*, ran the *AP*'s version in time for the next day's paper. In fact, the editors moved so quickly that they failed to get Wimbish's first name correct, calling him Robert instead of Ralph, confusing his first name with Dr. Swain's. The following day, various newspapers across the United States and Canada ran the *AP* story, from the *Portsmouth Daily Times* in Ohio to the *Edmonton Journal* in Alberta, Canada, to the *Milwaukee Journal*.

The *New York Times* took the lead on the story and began following up with other spring training host cities and hotels. In Sarasota, where the Chicago White Sox trained, hotel management indicated that there would be "little change in the practices of past years." That did not sit well with the Sox's owner, Bill Veeck. A rebel rouser and progressive thinker, Veeck responded that either the hotel management reconsiders its decision or he'd take his team elsewhere. The team's black players, including Minnie Minoso, would no longer be separated from the squad, Veeck declared, and when on the road, they would not be boarded in a segregated hotel. When the Sox were scheduled to play the Baltimore Orioles in Miami (where the Orioles trained), a representative from the visiting team's hotel informed the media that the White Sox "cancelled reservations because of a ban on Negro guests."

But the town of Sarasota, located thirty-five miles south of St. Petersburg and with a population of thirty-four thousand, had much more at stake than other spring training host cities. It was not a large metropolis like Miami (population of two hundred and ninety thousand), with a diversified economy that could weather the storm of a Major League Baseball team's departure. The following day, a spokesman from the Sarasota Chamber of Commerce announced that the White Sox would be able to have all of their players stay together at the team's hotel. It was a win for Veeck. He challenged the other owners to take a position on this issue: "[If] the owners make a united effort to break down segregation in the cities where their teams train, they will be successful."

Bill DeWitt, Cincinnati Reds co-owner and team general manager, based in Tampa, went on record that he wanted all of his players, including African American future Hall of Famer Frank Robinson, housed together if for no better reason than to be able to keep an eye on them.

Cleveland Indians star second baseman Larry Doby (later to be inducted into the Hall of Fame) added his voice to the cause. Recently retired, Doby, the second African American to play in the major leagues and the first to play in the American League, had firsthand experience playing in Florida. In 1959, Doby, at the end of his career, was traded to the Detroit Tigers in the off-season and sent to the team's spring training facility in nearby Lakeland, Florida. He was not welcomed by the fans. "I heard 'nigger' so many times in the outfield that I thought it was my middle name," as Doby remembered with a dose of sarcasm. In response to Wimbish's announcement, Doby went on record that he felt it was "the right time—exactly the right time—to fight it. Segregation is crumbling everywhere, so why not in baseball?"

Brooklyn Dodgers great Roy Campenella, who had been out of baseball since a 1958 car accident that left him paralyzed from the waist down, also spoke out. "If you play like a major leaguer, you should be permitted to live like one." His former boss, Branch Rickey, was one of the most vocal supporters of desegregation in sports and said, "It is an outrage. There is no earthly reason why Negro players shouldn't stay in the same hotels and eat in the same restaurants as other players." Just a few days after the article on Wimbish was published, Leon Lowery, the president of the Florida NAACP, sent letters to the involved thirteen major league teams asking them to stop patronizing segregated hotels. For the most part, Lowery's request fell on deaf ears. Actually, with few exceptions, the teams were doing their best to avoid the issue.

The Kansas City Athletics, who trained in West Palm Beach, did not have an immediate response. The World Champion Pittsburgh Pirates, who practiced in Fort Myers and whose players included outfielder Roberto Clemente, remained silent, as did the Philadelphia Phillies, who trained in nearby Clearwater.

"We have never had any trouble, and we don't expect any this year," said a Bradenton, Florida, city councilman, whose town hosted the Milwaukee Braves. The Braves featured one of the league's top home run hitters, Hank Aaron.

Although the mayor of Bradenton feared the housing issue "could put all cities in Florida" in danger of losing their spring training clubs, Birdie Tebbetts, the outspoken vice president of the Braves, played down the issue. In fact, he affirmed that his black players stayed in "carefully selected homes and . . . indicated complete satisfaction with the arrangements." That was not true. The previous spring, Aaron and black outfielders Wes Covington and Billy Bruton began to speak about the "daily inequities of spring training life." Aaron had also lobbied management to eliminate the segregated seating at its ballpark in Bradenton. The signs of "whites" and "colored" were an especially "humiliating reminder" to the players and their fans. The team ignored these requests.

Over the years, Aaron and his teammates stayed at the boarding house of Mrs. K.W. Gibson, "a tiny, gray-haired [African American] matron." Although they had nothing disrespectful to say about Gibson, her home was too small and inadequate for the number of grown men staying there. Their white teammates did not have to battle for hot showers. The team's traveling secretary, George Lewis, who coordinated logistics with Mrs. Gibson, pointed out that no one was "sleeping in the hall."

"They have nice rooms at Mrs. Gibson's," Lewis explained to the media. "She sets a fine table with plenty to eat. Why, I've been over there several times to eat myself."

While most of the teams' initial reactions were of indifference, some Floridians were outright angry about the desegregation effort. Days after the announcement was made, another cross was burned on the Wimbishs' front yard, followed by death threats. Dr. Swain was harassed as well.

"You are going to regret what you are doing," Elon C. Robison allegedly said to Swain by phone. The call came after Ellison's article about Wimbish was published. Known as "Robbie" to colleagues, Robison, who served as the city's vice mayor in the 1940s, was Al Lang's heir. He and Lang worked alongside each other, promoting St. Petersburg as the baseball training capital of the world. A falling out a year before Lang's death led many to believe that Robison would not be involved in baseball matters, but that was not the case. After Lang died,

Robison took over Lang's role as chairman of the city's Chamber of Commerce Baseball Committee and was appointed to the governor's statewide baseball committee. He even assumed the title of "Mr. Baseball."

Robison's anger probably had less to do with segregation and more to do with the potential economic hit for St. Petersburg and greater Florida. Spring training was a statewide, multi-million dollar enterprise. For St. Petersburg, in particular, it was also an integral part of the city's culture. "Baseball is the life blood of some of our communities," Robison explained to the media. "We can't upset the traditions of generations in a single day or a single year." What Robison feared most was Florida's spring training teams moving three thousand miles west to Arizona to join the Chicago Cubs, San Francisco Giants, Cleveland Indians, and Boston Red Sox.

When the four Arizona-based teams were asked about their situations, all of their representatives indicated that "they did not face the same problems." In Mesa, Arizona, where Ernie Banks and the Cubs held spring training, the team general manager made it clear that "everyone was welcome at the [team] hotel." In fact, he went so far as to "inform the people in [Arizona] cities that if Banks and our other African American players couldn't stay with the rest of the team, the team would not play." Ernie Banks may have been the most valuable player on the Cubs, but Willie Mays was indisputably the best all-around ballplayer to train in the Cactus League (if not the entire major league). Mays's team, the San Francisco Giants, who were based in Phoenix, hadn't experienced any issues of housing segregation either. Given that Yankees co-owner Del Webb lived and conducted business in Arizona, moving west was not out of the realm of possibility, at least for his team.

\*\*\*

"We're very much in favor of complete integration in baseball and of Elston Howard, Hector Lopez, and Jesse Gonder being allowed into the team hotel in St. Pete," New York Yankees co-owner Dan Topping told the *New York Post* syndicated columnist Milton Gross on February 1, 1961, the day after Wimbish's announcement. The team's publicity director, Bob Fishel, let it be known that the team was not sitting idle on the issue and efforts were being made to accommodate "all Yankee players who wanted to stay in the [Soreno] Hotel." The Soreno was only part of the problem, as evidenced by Elston Howard's concerns. In an interview with Gross, Howard expressed his thoughts on the issue for the first time:

I want to bring my family to training, just as the other Yankees [do], but I can't make plans until I get down there and see what kind of house I can rent. The other players can rent them from an agent in advance, but I can't [because of red line concerns]. It's not pleasant.

Even more unpleasant, the Soreno Hotel flatly refused to reconsider its segregationist policy. "We have always enjoyed having the New York Yankees with us. We hope to have them with us for many years to come on the same basis," the assistant hotel manager said on February 1. "I mean on the same basis as we've always had them by making arrangements for some of the players outside." That same day, Topping released his own statement to the press: "Howard, Lopez, and Gonder mean as much to our ball club as any other ball player, and we would like very much to have the whole team under one roof." It was the first time those three words—"under one roof"—were uttered. They took on a life of their own as other team representatives, players, and newsman used them to describe the housing segregation issue.

Both the *New York Times* and *New York Post* presumed that Topping's statement meant the Yankees were taking what "appeared to be the first step toward ending segregation." Baseball's commissioner Ford Frick and the American League president Joe Cronin offered their support to the team.

Unlike the Yanks, however, the Cards were unwilling to upset the status quo. "We recognize that it is highly desirable for all players to stay together," the Cardinals' general manager Bing Devine explained, "but we don't make the rules and regulations for the various localities." Perhaps Devine was anticipating the reaction from his white fan base back in Missouri if the team left St. Petersburg on the grounds of desegregation. Maybe he was working in tandem with the National League president, Warren Giles, who felt the housing issue was not a serious problem. It was an ironic twist of events since Devine's club fielded three black starters and the National League was much more progressive regarding the sport's integration than the American League. At this time, there were twice as many African Americans in the National League than in the American League, which would play a key role in the National League's future domination.

On February 3, 1961, the day after Topping's "under one roof" announcement, C.H. Alberdine, the president of the Tulsa, Oklahoma, company that owned the Soreno and Vinoy Park hotels, stated his position on the issue:

When either the Yankees or the Cardinals, or both, feel the situation has developed so they must insist on housing all their personnel in the same hotel, then the Yankees and the Cardinals should look for other hotels.

Florida Governor C. Farris Bryant, who had taken office a month earlier, was brought into the debate. An experienced politician, Bryant lived up to his reputation. Sidestepping the issue, he pointed out that although teams who insisted on housing their African American players in the hotels would be in violation of local customs, it did not constitute breaking the law. Bryant avoided offending either of the teams whom his state's economy depended on or the local businesses whose support he needed during election time.

Facing an uphill battle, Topping and the Yankees' public relations director, Bob Fishel, informed the media that even though their team "made more of an effort than any other club," (which was not accurate, given the actions by Veeck), nothing more would be done at this year's spring training.

# 7

# YANKEES' DEPARTURE

"The announcement came as though by accident during a press conference concerning another matter," the *St. Petersburg Times* reported on February 4, 1961. It was the day after Dan Topping went on record stating that there was "not a thing the team could do about" the segregated housing policy at his team's hotel.

After most of the reporters had already left the press conference, one of the few who stuck around asked Topping about the situation in Florida. His response was far different than his previous one. To the shock of the handful of assembled journalists, Topping announced that the Yankees might be leaving St. Petersburg.

"In St. Petersburg, we practice on one field and play on

another. There is too much jumping around," Topping explained further. "The colored situation has nothing do with it but we have been contacted by people from Fort Lauderdale. They have proposed building certain facilities. . . . [If] they do [build a stadium], the chances are we'll move from St. Petersburg."

The city of Fort Lauderdale, located two hundred and fifty miles southeast, near Miami, had offered to build an eight thousand-seat stadium, complete with air-conditioned locker rooms and onsite staff offices, neither of which was available at Al Lang Stadium. There were plenty of luxury hotels for the team to stay in and all of them allowed African Americans. "We have nothing against St. Petersburg. But at Fort Lauderdale, we would have a town and park all to ourselves instead of sharing it with the St. Louis Cardinals."

A reporter asked when the Yankees would depart from the Sunshine City. The Yankees' agreement with St. Petersburg did not expire until the beginning of 1963, but in the team's contract there was a "one-year escape clause," which meant if another team was willing to train in St. Petersburg, the Yankees could leave a year earlier than contractually allowed without penalty.

Unfortunately for the Yanks, since many of the other teams had their own agreements and did not have an escape clause, it seemed unlikely that the option was viable. Even if a team was interested in moving, why would it switch to St. Petersburg and endure Jim Crow? By 1961, every team had at least one African American player on its roster and many of them were stars.

"We intend to live up to our contract," Topping maintained. "No move would be possible until after the 1962 spring [season]."

Despite Topping's initial assertion that racial restrictions did not play a role in his decision, the issue of Jim Crow housing was raised once again. "Our position in the matter of segregation of players has been made and is known," he stated. "I repeat that I would like very much to have the whole team under one roof." On the other hand, according to the *St. Petersburg Times*, Topping "took pains to declare that the decision [was] in no way related to segregation problems."

In private, the Yankees' co-owner let it be known that he felt St. Petersburg had become a "dead city." Members of the team, he said, had confided to management that they found the town "depressing" and overrun with sixty-five-year-old shuffleboard players. Besides everyone in the media and inside baseball circles knew that Topping's yacht and winter home were based in Fort Lauderdale, the "Venice of America," as the *New York Times* nicknamed it.

While these considerations help in part to explain the impending Yankees' departure, the reasons why Topping refused to acknowledge directly the race issue remains a mystery. Even the team's publicity director, Bob Fishel, admitted that desegregation was a "definite plus" when it came to his boss's decision to move.

In Dr. Wimbish's view, it was perfectly obvious why the Pinstripes were leaving St. Petersburg. Unable to house their players in one place, they had no choice. As for the team's public explanation, according to Wimbish, it was hardly convincing. "The expressed reason is that they will have Fort Lauderdale to themselves, instead of continuing to share St. Pete with the Cardinals. The Yankees were here with the Cards for a long time before Fort Lauderdale suddenly seemed more attractive."

The St. Petersburg Baseball Committee chairman was "disturbed" over the rapid turn of events. For E.C. Robison, the departure of the Yankees was the second-worst possible outcome (the worst: both teams leaving St. Petersburg). During the previous spring training, a study was conducted of St. Petersburg's tourism industry. The results indicated that more than two-thirds of visitors who had been polled cited baseball as their number-one reason for visiting The Sunshine City. And if the Yankees left, what would be the immediate fiscal impact?

While Robison, local political officials, and the business community went into mourning, there were those who were jubilant over the Yankees' decision—none more so than Wendell Smith.

From Veeck's victory in Sarasota and his courageous stand in Miami to the Yankees' decision to depart St. Petersburg, the journalist took much of the credit for these developments, failing to recognize the pivotal role played by Wimbish.

Whatever ill feelings that might have produced, the task at hand superseded them. Both Smith and Wimbish realized that the struggle for equal housing was far from over. The majority of teams who trained in Florida were adamant about "not rocking the boat" when it came to putting demands on their host cities and hotels.

Kansas City Athletics general manager Frank Lane, for instance, told the *New York Times*, "[We] are not spearheading any political movements. . . . If it has been accepted in the past that Negroes use different hotels, then we have to subscribe to what has been done in the past."

"My boys do not mind being subjected to the Jim Crow laws in the spring," Milwaukee Braves vice president Birdie Tebbetts incorrectly asserted. "They are happy, perfectly satisfied with their lowly status."

Proclamations by Lane and Tebbetts, no matter how unpopular among black players, drew little attention. All eyes were on The Sunshine City. Whatever happened in St. Petersburg would determine the course of events throughout Florida. If the Vinoy Park Hotel, where the Cardinals stayed, surrendered to integration, it would set a precedent. "[We] would have followed suit," an unidentified hotel manager from another spring training host town confided to a reporter for the *New York Times*.

That spring Wendell Smith and Sam Lacy, Jr., his former colleague at the *Pittsburgh Courier*, penned two-dozen articles about baseball's housing crisis. Smith reminded the teams that it was *they* who wielded the power. The cities and hotels were at the teams' whim, not the other way around. "It so happens that the sun shines just as bright in the West as it does in Florida's tropical communities," Smith contended. Whether it was Arizona or southern California, Jim Crow would not be an issue. "They [city officials who hosted teams during spring training] should seriously contemplate what a baseball exodus could mean to the entire state of Florida, as well as their own communities."

Robison got the message. In an interview with the *New York Times*, he admitted that spring training was more important to Florida's economy than maintaining Southern traditions. The writing was on the wall. Why risk the loss of any team over a policy that inevitably would be overturned?

Other sacred segregated institutions in St. Petersburg were crumbling. The all-white hospital, Mound Park, was under siege. Dr. Wimbish and his African American colleagues demanded full desegregation of the facility. Anxious to avoid further confrontation, the city council proposed a multi-million dollar bond expansion project at all-black Mercy Hospital, which was rejected by Wimbish and the NAACP. Then the council offered to build a separate wing for people of color at Mound Park, which was opposed by the white community. Frustrated, city officials came up with what they considered to be the only workable solution.

Dr. Fred Alsup recalled how it went down. "They told me that once you get the first black over there [Mound Park Hospital] and open it up, it won't be any problem." As far as city officials were concerned, there was no need for further discussion.

On February 26, 1961, Ms. Altamese Chapman, an African American resident, entered Mound Park Hospital through the front doors accompanied by Dr. Alsup. No one blocked the entryway or the hallway. The hospital staff was accommodating to Dr. Alsup and Ms. Chapman, who was treated for varicose veins. Her stay lasted for one week. The press was informed that Ms. Chapman was the first African American admitted to Mound Park and Dr. Alsup was the first physician to admit a black patient. From that moment on, Mound Park Hospital served both black and white residents.

Closer to home, Dr. Wimbish's daughter, fifteen-year-old Barbara, became the first African American student to attend the local, all-girls Catholic high school, St. Paul. Although she resisted at first, preferring the neighborhood public school where her friends attended, Barbara acquiesced, a result of her mother's subtle persuasion. With the exception of one student who made life difficult for her at St. Paul, most of her fellow white students were "very nice," and it turned out to be a pleasant experience.

If Wimbish's and Topping's announcements and the desegregation of other St. Petersburg facilities were not enough to rattle the nerves of St. Petersburg's baseball establishment, a third issue emerged before the teams even played their first exhibition game of spring training.

On March 8, 1961, the day before the St. Petersburg Chamber of Commerce's "Salute to Baseball" annual breakfast at the St. Petersburg Yacht Club, Joe Reichler of the *Associated Press* met with the Cardinals' Bill White. Reichler was well respected by baseball players, especially African Americans.[1] Reichler and another reporter, Howard Cosell, a lawyer and radio sportscaster, were viewed by the players as the only white journalists at the time who spoke about racism in professional sports.

---

1. Joe Reichler was so respected that, in 1966, he was hired by Major League Baseball to serve as the Director of Publicity in the Office of the Commissioner.

The St. Petersburg Yacht Club.

When Reichler asked White about the breakfast, the first baseman was stumped. He hadn't been aware of the event. He hadn't been invited. White became furious when he learned that Doug Clemens, a white, "rookie outfielder who had never swung a bat in the major leagues" was invited to the breakfast. White let loose:

I can't stay at the same hotel as the white players. These players are my friends, yet I can't go swimming with them. I can't even go to the movies with them. Driving on the highways, I've got to be on the lookout for a Negro restaurant to eat because they won't let me in where the white folks eat.... These things go on every day and yet they advise us to take it easy, we're making progress, don't push it too fast, it will come. How much longer are we to wait? When will we be made to feel like humans?

His lengthy diatribe ran in every newspaper in the country that subscribed to the *AP* wire. All of a sudden this routine celebration breakfast "became a national news story." In a span of less than six weeks, baseball and St. Petersburg were under fire again.

The media bombarded the St. Louis Cardinals' public relations director Jim Toomey with questions. Why was White not invited? Were any black players invited? What about the Yankees? Did the yacht club have a ban against blacks?

Player invitations were based on "convenience to the location of the breakfast only," Toomey said, trying to quell the media storm. What he really meant was that if a player was not staying at the hotel, which was less than a fifteen-minute walk to the St Petersburg Yacht Club, he hadn't been invited. "Not all ballplayers are eager to get up early in the morning to attend a breakfast," Toomey explained. "I only listed the players staying at the Vinoy Park Hotel."

Technically, not every white ball player stayed at the Vinoy. The team's other first baseman, the aging Stan Musial, had brought his family to St. Petersburg and stayed at a condo that was more conducive to his needs. According to the team, Musial and four other white baseball players who did not stay at the hotel were not invited to the breakfast either.

To no one's surprise, Wendell Smith threw himself in the debate. When Toomey said he tried to get in touch with White and the other African American players on the team (i.e., Curt Flood and Bob Gibson) but was unsuccessful, Smith called the Cardinals' public relations director a liar. The uproar over the club breakfast caused a St. Louis-based African American newspaper to call for a boycott of Anheuser-Busch beer, the Cardinals' owner Gussie Busch's family-owned business.

The Yankees handled this issue far better than the Cardinals. Management put a "blanket invitation" on the players' bulletin board at the team's practice field, but given the uproar,

Elston Howard still assumed that he was not invited. According to the Yankees' public relations director Bob Fishel, the catcher approached him, holding the invitation, and asked, "Does this mean me?" Fishel responded, "Everyone."

The organizer of the breakfast tried to place blame on the teams, citing that it was their responsibility to coordinate the event with the players. "We invited baseball players—not colors," the St. Petersburg Chamber of Commerce's president explained. "There is absolutely no reason why Bill White and other Negro players could not take part. This is a personal invitation to White himself and all other Negro players on the two teams."

When Bill White discussed the matter with Bette Wimbish and his teammate Curt Flood at the Wimbish home, both of them encouraged him to attend, hoping it would "break down the barriers." White wouldn't budge. "Why should I wake up at six in the morning to eat breakfast with a bunch of racists?"

In the end, neither White nor Flood attended. Of the forty-eight players who went to the breakfast on March 9, only one was African American—Elston Howard.

***

Since 1957, when the Giants left Manhattan for San Francisco, and the Dodgers pulled out of Brooklyn for Los Angeles, New York City had been home to only one baseball team. That was about to change with the introduction of the New York Mets.

During the tumultuous spring of 1961, the Mets were still a year away from their inaugural season, but personnel decisions were already underway. On March 14, the former Yankees' general manager George Weiss was hired to serve as president of the Mets. It was an odd arrangement of sorts. His new office was only four blocks south of his old one, and on top of what he was paid by the Mets, he still received from his former employer an annual salary of $35,000 (equivalent of $275,000 in 2015) for the next five years as part of his severance.

Weiss's first order of business was to find a location for the Mets' spring training. One could imagine all of the cities representing Florida and Arizona lobbying the former Yankees' general manager to select them as the home for baseball's newest team in America's largest media market. What no one knew, though, was that Weiss was already involved in negotiations.

It was presumed the Yankees would spend at least one more season in St. Petersburg. Topping and Weiss had other plans. On March 21, the Yankees' owners confirmed that their team would not be training in St. Petersburg the following season, which technically was a violation of their agreement, but that same day, at another press conference, the city's Baseball Committee chairman, Robison, announced that St. Petersburg had a new tenant—the New York Mets—and the Yankees were formally released from their contractual obligations. The Pinstripes were not completely abandoning The Sunshine City, though. Yankees co-owner Del Webb informed the press that the team was planning to build a training facility in St. Petersburg (on 1,400 acres, all owned by Webb's construction company) for the team's minor league operation. It was not equal to having a professional team present during the spring, but it was better than no Yankees' presence at all.

# 8

# THE FALLOUT

Six months after Dr. Wimbish delivered his historic announcement calling for St. Petersburg to end segregated housing during spring training, the players took up the issue on August 1 at the annual Major League Baseball Players Association (MLBPA) meeting in Boston. Although neither served as their official MLBPA team representative, Bill White and Detroit Tigers' centerfielder Billy Bruton were present to discuss the housing controversy, but even before the meeting took place, White made his position clear. "If the players are going to pussyfoot over this thing I'd just as soon not attend the meeting," White told Frank Scott, the director of MLBPA. "If they are serious about doing something and really want to hear our side of the problem, then I will be glad to cooperate."

The MLBPA was led by Scott and Milwaukee-based judge Robert Cannon, both of whom were avid supporters of integrated housing. "I am convinced that every white major leaguer views this problem with deep sympathy," Cannon responded when asked about the MLBPA's stance. "[We] will be willing to support the grievances of the Negro players when they are presented at the meeting." One way or the other, Cannon pointed out, it was "an issue which baseball [could not] dodge."

The eighteen MLBPA representatives supported White and Bruton unanimously, sending a message to Major League Baseball that players would not stay in hotels or play in stadiums where segregation was enforced during the spring training season. To gauge where matters stood, Scott and Cannon sent a letter asking for "a brief summary of [each team's] situation with respect to housing all players under one roof during Spring Training." The first teams to respond promptly had already resolved the issue or did not have a problem with segregation in the first place.

"You folks must be out of your mind," wrote a representative from the Los Angles Dodgers, which was the first team to have integrated quarters during spring training in Vero Beach, Florida. "We eat, sleep and drink under the same roof. That is the only reason we train at Dodgertown. . . . Now get lost!" Team owner Walter O'Malley admitted in a separate letter that relations with local officials in Vero Beach were not as "cordial" as the team would have liked.

The teams based in Arizona—the Chicago Cubs, San Francisco Giants, and Cleveland Indians—responded with brief letters acknowledging that their teams provided the same accommodations for white and black players during spring training. The Los Angeles Angels, who trained in Palm Springs, California, and would begin their first season the following year, did not experience problems, either. However, the team's general manager noted that during a recent traveling exhibition game to Atlanta, the team was forced to send their black players to a different hotel.

*Yankees' catcher Elston Howard looks at the call of the umpire during Game 2 of the 1961 World Series, played October 5, 1961 at Yankee Stadium. Photograph from "Baseball Digest," front cover, December 1961-Janurary 1962 issue and distributed under a CC-BY 2.0 license.*

The Yankees' new general manager, Roy Hamey, was also an early responder. The officials of Fort Lauderdale, reported

Hamey, were thrilled to host the Yanks the next season. The "luckiest city in the nation" was how they described themselves in view of their good fortune. The team moved into the Yankee Clipper, which looked more like a cruise ship than a team hotel. For the most part, there was no segregation in Fort Lauderdale as Arlene Howard, Elston's widow, recalled. "It was quite nice. Everything was open including beaches, restaurants."

Hector Lopez concurred, having fond memories of the town, especially of bringing his spouse Claudette and socializing with his teammates in the same dining room. Yankee pitcher Al Downing viewed it differently. Downing, an African American, who was in his first full season with the club and hadn't experienced St. Petersburg, recalled being told by team management that he, Howard, and Lopez had to use a side door when entering the Clipper dining room. They pushed back. One day, the three men decided to enter the dinning room through the hotel's main lobby. No one from the hotel or team put up resistance. From then on, no part of the Clipper was off limits. Still, Downing recalled, segregation remained largely the law of the land throughout Florida until the early 1970s.

Although the Yankees got off to a poor start in spring training of 1961, going 1–8, Ralph Houk, their new manager settled in and soon realized the team's overwhelming advantage with Mantle and Maris in the lineup. The two sluggers battled it out in the most exciting single-season home run race ever, with Maris victorious, setting a new MLB single-season record. He had sixty-one home runs, one more than the Babe. The Yankees went on to have one of the best seasons in team history, culminating in their World Series victory over the Cincinnati Reds.

The Chicago White Sox's general manager and Hall of Fame slugger, Hank Greenberg, explained that the team was "making every effort" to locate integrated quarters. The team had a new owner, Chicago-based banker Arthur C. Allyn, who purchased the team from Bill Veeck. Although the new owner may have been more reserved than his "flamboyant" predecessor, Allyn was equally committed to ending segregated housing for spring training. Later that fall, the White Sox paid $500,000 for the purchase of the 117-room Sarasota Terrace Hotel, where the team previously stayed, ensuring that all players were under one roof.

Another Florida-based team, the Baltimore Orioles, also had resolved the issue. Their assistant general manager worked out an agreement with the city of Miami where the team trained. The hotel accommodating the Orioles would be fully integrated for the 1962 season.

The Milwaukee Braves' vice president Birdie Tebbetts responded that the team had not yet finalized quarters for the upcoming season. Tebbetts had always insisted that his black players were perfectly satisfied with the housing situation. Later that year, he apparently changed his mind, announcing that the Braves were moving their spring training site from Bradenton to Palmetto, only two miles north. At its new facility and hotel, the team was promised that all of the athletes would be able to live and eat together.

Teams who had either made no attempt or failed to come to an agreement with their host cities were slower to respond to the MLBPA's request. Kansas City Athletics General Manager Frank Lane, for example, wrote that his team's host city, West Palm Beach, Florida, did not have a hotel willing to accommodate all of the players and the team was not planning to change its policy for the 1962 season. However, the following year, the team moved to Bradenton, where it found integrated housing.

The Minnesota Twins (formerly the Washington Senators) acknowledged that they had not resolved the segregated housing of their players. Based in Orlando, the Twins claimed that due to local customs, "[It had] not made any effort to house and feed [its] negro players at the same hotel . . . [and felt it] should not get further involved with the local attitudes in the Southern states." In 1964, the Twins integrated its quarters, the last team to do so.

The Philadelphia Phillies placed the onus on the hotel's manager who argued that the people of the area dictated the hotel's policy. By the start of the 1962 season, the fans back home had demanded integrated quarters in Clearwater, Florida, where the Phillies trained. The Philadelphia chapter of the NAACP threatened to boycott the team's home games if change was not imminent. Under mounting pressure, the Phillies let it be known that if it couldn't get accommodations under one roof in Clearwater, it would try another area. The town and hotel took the threat seriously and capitulated to the team's demands.

The Detroit Tigers, according to Wendell Smith, was the

one club in Florida least committed to desegregation. A team representative claimed that it had "made every effort to house all of their players under one roof in Lakeland," but that local officials rejected all proposals. Instead of moving to a different city, the team accepted the officials' decision. Finally, in 1963, under a new general manager, the team found different living quarters in Lakeland that readily admitted their black players.

At the time of the MLBPA meeting, St. Petersburg had yet to resolve the housing status of the Mets and Cardinals. Wendell Smith believed that the Mets, under George Weiss's leadership, "had formed a segregation pact with the city." If that were the case, he wanted New Yorkers to demand their tax-funded stadium dollars back from their city. Smith's call-to-action was premature. In the end, the Mets opted not to use the Soreno Hotel (the former Yankee stomping ground) and instead took up residence at the Colonial Inn (still in St. Petersburg), where all seven of the team's African American players were allowed to stay. For their inaugural season, the Mets had recruited another ex-Yankee, Casey Stengel, to serve as their manager.

The St. Louis Cardinals' general manager, Bing Devine, informed the MLBPA that the team had met with city and hotel officials. Hoping to come to an agreement soon, Devine acknowledged that management was "cognizant of the undesirable conditions" for the black players. Unlike the Yankees, however, the Cardinals had no plans to leave St. Petersburg. If their demands were not met, they would have to take matters into their own hands, and they did.

In July 1961, manager Solly Hemus was fired. His record was unimpressive and his behavior toward African American players was often cruel. To the players, especially White, Flood, and Gibson, the firing was a sign that management was on their side. The team was unable to come to an agreement with the Vinoy Park Hotel. In 1962, the team found new living quarters at the Doctors Motel (later known as the Outrigger Inn) in St. Petersburg, a recently built two-story, nondescript motel located near the Sunshine Skyway. Unlike the Vinoy, the team had full control of its quarters since the motel was owned by Busch's friends. Nearly all of the players and their families stayed there that season, even Stan Musial, who normally maintained a private residence. It was such a novelty in St. Petersburg to have an integrated hotel that the team's residence soon became a "local tourist attraction," as recalled by African American pitcher Bob Gibson. "People would drive by to see the white and black families swimming together," including Musial's and White's families. Bill White described it as "our own little civil rights movement." Meanwhile, the team's former hotel fell on hard times.

Compounded with a declining downtown and an aging infrastructure—the ballroom, for example, was being used as a volleyball court—the once-glamorous Vinoy Park Hotel closed its doors in 1974. Thereafter, the hotel sat dormant and was set to be torn down until city residents voted to save it in 1984. Eventually, it was purchased by a private investor and underwent a $100 million renovation before it reopened its doors in 1992. Today, the Vinoy Park Hotel thrives and is once again the centerpiece of Beach Drive. In 2016, it celebrated its ninetieth anniversary.

Unfortunately, the Soreno, where the Yankees stayed during spring training for more than twenty-five years, did not fare as well. Like the Vinoy, the aging Soreno was not properly maintained, and it closed in 1984. But unlike its counterpart down the street, the Soreno was not saved. In 1992, in the action film *Lethal Weapon 3*, the hotel was intentionally destroyed during a scene when an explosive device was detonated.

Whatever the impact the Yankees departure might have had on the demise of the Soreno, one thing is certain. After the Yanks left St. Petersburg, it was no longer the pinnacle team in the majors. In 1964, pitcher Bob Gibson led the Cardinals to beat the Yankees and win the World Series. It was the beginning of the end of the Yankees' dynasty, and it would be thirteen more years before the Pinstripes were victorious again in October.

Bill White, one of the few players in baseball history to earn a .300 batting average and drive in one hundred runs for three consecutive seasons, may be better known for his post-playing career. For nearly a decade, White worked with ex-Yank Phil Rizuto as a New York Yankees' broadcaster, becoming the first African American to regularly do the play-by-play announcing for a professional sports team.

In 1989, White was named president of the National League. His five-year tenure was fraught with controversy, leading the *New York Times* to call him "Baseball's Angry Man." In 1992, White refused to support St. Petersburg's bid for a Major

League Baseball franchise, something it had been requesting for more than decade. Incensed, city officials and residents accused White of seeking revenge for how he had been treated during his spring training days with the Cardinals. White insisted that his opposition was not based on past wrongs, simply on the economics of the situation, arguing that St. Petersburg did not have the financial base to support a Major League Baseball franchise.

A year after White left office, St. Petersburg in 1995 was awarded its coveted team, the Tampa Bay Devil Rays. In 1998, the Rays played their first season at Tropicana Field, a non-retractable dome stadium located in the Gas Plant district where Wimbish grew up. After the stadium had been built, Terry Wimbish, an attorney and the youngest of the three Wimbish children, voiced his frustration to a reporter for the Tampa-based weekly newspaper, *Creative Loafing*. "There are several reasons why I do not like *that* Dome." In order to accommodate its construction, he explained, the Gas Plant neighborhood was razed, and the residents—overwhelmingly African American—were displaced.

Since the team's inception, the Rays have experienced mixed results. Although the team made it to the 2008 World Series where it lost to the Phillies and, until 2013, had been one of the top teams in the American League, it has consistently had one of the lowest MLB attendance records. As a consequence, the Rays' owner is, as of the spring of 2016, lobbying the city of St. Petersburg to allow his team to relocate across the bay in Tampa. In addition to having a larger population and economy,

Tampa is more centrally located within the region and some believe can better support the team.

Al Lang Stadium is now home to the Tampa Bay Rowdies, a professional year-round soccer team. Baseball is no longer played at the historic field.

As for Al Lang Field, until 1987, the New York Mets continued to hold spring training at the oceanfront ballpark. Starting in 1991, the Baltimore Orioles trained at Al Lang for four seasons. When the Rays entered the league in 1998, the team held spring training there, but that ended in 2008. Since then, no MLB team has regularly used Al Lang Field, which is now referred to as Al Lang Stadium. The sports park currently hosts the Tampa Bay Rowdies, a men's professional soccer team, whose owner brokered an agreement with the City of St. Petersburg that the stadium would not to be used for baseball games or practices. Aside from a few copper plaques scattered throughout the front entrances and the logos of the eight Major League Baseball teams that called the field home plastered on an obscure wall below a couple of soccer posters, there are no traces of its baseball past.

No longer holding a near-monopoly, Florida's Grapefruit League gave up ground to Arizona's Cactus League. Spring training for Major League Baseball's thirty teams is now evenly split between the two states. Baseball experts believe that Arizona's more predictable weather and economic enticements will inevitably pave the way to Arizona hosting the majority of teams during spring training.

# 9

# EPILOGUE

The struggle for racial justice in St. Petersburg did not end with the integration of baseball's spring training. The goal for Ralph Wimbish and the NAACP was to eradicate "all references to segregation," legal or otherwise.

When Bill White and Bob Gibson were in town, they joined Wimbish for dinner at a number of the city's restaurants or bars that were known for catering only to whites. Dressed in fine attire, the players would meet with Wimbish beforehand, and he would inform them of the plan which typically went like: "Tonight, we're going to integrate this restaurant" or "Tonight, we're going to this white-only club." During those outings, the three men encountered little to no resistance, and they were never denied service. Bill White started calling Wimbish "the devil" because of all "the hell he raised."

With Bette at his side, the couple was instrumental in the launch of a massive effort four years in the making that resulted in the desegregation of St. Petersburg's schools. In addition, Wimbish and Dr. Alsup challenged Pinellas County over a lease agreement that enabled the private operators of a golf course on county-owned land to discriminate against people of color. It was dragged through the courts and ended up in the US Federal Court of Appeals, which sided with the plaintiffs.

In addition to these causes, Wimbish was engaged in a never-ending battle with the city's biracial committee, made up of appointed black and white citizens, for its failure to address discriminatory employment practices at the city hall and in the local private sector.

No longer the president of the NAACP, Wimbish resumed the leadership of the Ambassadors Club. Frequently selected as the keynote speaker at banquets, meetings, and memorials, Wimbish was viewed by the local black community as its most effective advocate. Even when he accused his fellow African Americans of not doing their fair share—"We can't entirely blame the white community for what is our lot," he said in a 1963 church sermon—his followers never lost faith.

As he entered his forties, Wimbish's pace remained relentless. Quelling stress with an addictive cigarette habit did not improve matters. Although he continued his routine of leaving work to go home for lunch and a quick nap, the energetic physician spent most of the day at his medical office or engaged with the activities of the NAACP and the Ambassadors Club. When he was home, his evenings and early mornings were usually interrupted by patients' requests for house calls. Unfortunately, he did not heed his daughter's warnings, "Daddy, you need to stop smoking those things," which, coupled with his exhaustive routine, would undoubtedly have an impact on his health.

Blessed with boundless drive and ambition, Bette Wimbish was not far behind her husband. In 1965, once the children were older, Bette returned to school seeking a law degree. She had applied to Stetson University College of Law, which was only a ten minute drive from her home. Unfortunately, Stetson, Florida's first law school, was still segregated and did not accept Bette. It would be six more years before the law school admitted its first African American student. With no other option, Bette applied and was accepted to her alma mater, Florida A&M. Since its law school was located in Tallahassee, about two hundred and fifty miles north of St. Petersburg, it created a problem for the family. The oldest child, Barbara, an undergraduate at Howard University, was independent, but Ralph Jr. and Terry were still in school. It was decided that Bette and her sons would live in Tallahassee while Wimbish stayed behind in St. Petersburg, with visits home scheduled once a month and during holidays.

Consequently, Bette did her best to "zip through law school in just two and half years, all the while attending to the daily needs [of her two boys]." Two weeks before Bette's final exams, the family had scheduled a weekend vacation in Miami for

Florida A&M's annual Orange Blossom Classic football game. Missing his dad and friends, Ralph Jr. had convinced his parents to let him move back to St. Petersburg and live with his father.

On December 1, 1967, the morning of the planned vacation, Dr. Wimbish woke up and told his son that his tongue was bleeding. Once father and son arrived at the Four Ambassadors hotel in Miami, Wimbish met with an old friend and former Meharry classmate, Dr. John Brown. After a brief check-up by Dr. Brown, Wimbish and his son went about their day and later picked up Bette and Terry from the airport. Barbara, who was living with her husband, Eric Griffin, in Boston, did not make the trip. By the time the family got back to the hotel, it was almost midnight.

Soon after midnight, Ralph Jr., deep asleep, was woken to the sounds of his mother screaming. "Paralyzed by fear, I couldn't get out of bed," he recalled. Bette continued to yell and scream while she tried to save her husband who was suffering a heart attack. The paramedics arrived and took him to the hospital. Bette ran over to Ralph Jr., sobbing, "I'm sorry, I'm sorry. I tried to save him. He had a heart attack. I'm sorry." When Ralph Wimbish arrived at the hospital, he was pronounced dead. He was forty-five years old.

The funeral for Dr. Wimbish was held at his longtime place of worship, First Baptist Institutional Church. Chrystelle Stewart, the former A&M college classmate, recalled that it was "the first time [the church] had a full house," standing room only. The death of Dr. Wimbish, in Mrs. Stewart's words, was "a blow to St. Petersburg"—a sentiment shared by many, particularly in the black community.

***

Two weeks after her husband's death and a week following the funeral, Bette drove back to Tallahassee to take her final exams. Despite the emotional trauma and heartache, Bette managed to pass her exams and, in 1968, passed the Florida bar exam.

Having moved back to St. Petersburg, Bette set up a law practice in her husband's former medical office, next door to the apartment and commercial complex that was known as the "Wimbish Building." She earned a reputation as a staunch legal advocate for the city's African American community, and in 1969, she ran for a seat on the St. Petersburg City Council. She was successful. Bette became the first person of color in St. Petersburg to serve in that capacity.

Like her late husband, Bette fought to alter the city's pro-white hiring and promotion policies. She was also responsible for ending the "tradition of council members eating lunch together at the then-segregated [St. Petersburg] Yacht Club on council meeting days," the same club that Bill White complained about to the national media nearly a decade earlier. In the midst of all this activity, Bette remarried.

In 1971, Bette was elevated to vice mayor. Her council term ended the following year, and rather than run for reelection, she launched a bid to become a state senator. Although she lost the race, she was later appointed by Florida Governor

Reuben Askew (a Democrat) to be the associate director of the Division of Labor and Employment Opportunities of the Department of Commerce. Later, Bette became the deputy secretary of commerce. Politically ambitious, she ran for elected office on two more occasions without success. She was also screened for a seat on the Florida State Supreme Court, but it did not materialize.

After her youngest child, Terry, died in 1993 at thirty-two years-old from AIDS, her political aspirations waned, and she worked as a lawyer for the Florida Department of Social Services. Bette Wimbish retired in 1999 and died in 2009 at the age of eighty-five.

Her daughter, Barbara, graduated from Howard and married in 1967 at the Outrigger Inn. She and her husband Eric settled in St. Petersburg where she worked as a social worker and raised a family. One of her two children, Jennifer, followed in her grandfather's footsteps and became a doctor. An obstetrician/gynecologist, Jennifer currently practices in St. Petersburg and, coincidentally, enjoys playing piano on the same piano as her grandfather had decades earlier. Barbara's son, Eurich, is a graduate of Morehouse College.

At the age of eleven, Ralph Jr. carried out the family tradition when he integrated the city's all-white Little League. As a teenager, Ralph Jr. served as copyboy at the *St. Petersburg Times*, where many of the staff, including Jack Ellison, the journalist who broke the story of Wimbish's historic announcement, had known his father. Ralph Jr. continued to work in that newsroom while attending the University of South Florida in

Tampa. After graduation, he had a successful career with several publications, including the *Pittsburgh Post-Gazette*, *Golf Digest*, and the *New York Post*. In 2001, he co- authored a memoir, *Elston and Me: The Story of the First Black Yankee*, with Elston's widow, Arlene Howard.

Holding a photograph of Dr. Wimbish, the author poses with his children, Barbara Griffin and Ralph Wimbish, Jr., during a visit to St. Petersburg.

\*\*\*

Mordecai Walker, who was a pallbearer at Wimbish's funeral, remembered that after Dr. Wimbish died, "no one stepped up to lead the fight." As a result, the civil rights movement in St. Petersburg "slowed down." In the Twenty-Second Street South neighborhood, the Wimbish Building still stands but is in a dilapidated state. The ground floor, which was originally home to a black-owned pharmacy, is now leased as a liquor store. At Mercy Hospital (now Bayfront Medical Center), there is a civil rights exhibit in the main lobby that includes a life-size mannequin of Dr. Fred Alsup and a collage of photographs that feature Drs. Alsup, Ayer, Ponder, and Wimbish. In 2014, the city erected a series of historic markers that were placed along the sidewalks of Twenty-Second Street South to honor active African American residents from the community. The marker that features Dr. and Mrs. Wimbish is placed in front of the hospital.

The Wimbish home or "Wimbish Hotel" once stood ten blocks from the hospital. In the 1970s, through eminent domain, the city approved the destruction of all homes and businesses that stood in the way of the future interstate highway, I-275. Plans for the location of the highway ran right through the middle of the Twenty-Second Street South neighborhood, displacing hundreds of families and causing scores of businesses from the once vibrant neighborhood to close. Bette Wimbish, according to Ralph Jr., fought the injunction but lost. Instead of getting torn down, their seven-room pink house was moved to Pinellas Park and became a home for priests. Tough times for the community ensued for several decades afterward.

The Wimbish Building in its current state. It is no longer owned by the Wimbish family.

The iconic Southside neighborhood, though, has experienced a recent, yet painfully slow reemergence. Along with the addition of the historic markers, there are new developments taking place, such as the renovation of the live entertainment venue Manhattan Casino, the establishment of a New Orleans-style café called Chief Creole, and a new junior college satellite campus. The neighborhood has even been granted a new name: Midtown. However, the scars left from segregation and urban renewal remain.

***

While looking back at the integration of spring training, "All of this came about because a Negro doctor in St. Petersburg, Dr. Ralph Wimbish, spoke up," Elston Howard told Jackie Robinson. Ralph Wimbish "had guts," Bill White recalled in an interview with the author. "He had no fear [and was a] man ahead of his times." Elston Howard's widow, Arlene, remembered Dr. Wimbish as a "real fighter for civil rights." Former *St. Petersburg Times* reporter Sam Adams, who followed Wimbish's role in the community, could not have agreed more. He insisted that Wimbish was the "key man" ending segregated housing in spring training and leading the city's civil rights movement.

Even Alex Haley's taxi driver, while he drove the journalist around St. Petersburg, expressed strongly that "Dr. Wimbish had a whole lot to do with" the changes that affected spring training and the welfare of the region's black community. Hank Aaron summarized the spring training situation best: "[T]here wasn't a white man in Florida—or in baseball, for that matter—who was going to change things just out of his sense of decency. It had to happen through pressure."

No one applied that pressure more effectively than Dr. Ralph Wimbish. How many people, as Ralph Jr. put it wryly, could claim to have driven the New York Yankees out of town? To be sure, Dr. Wimbish had help: his wife, friends, colleagues, the players, sympathetic baseball executives, and the stinging columns written by Wendell Smith. At the apex of the movement, however, Wimbish stood valiantly.

Dr. Wimbish seems largely forgotten in St. Petersburg now.

Most of his contemporaries have either died or are in their eighties and nineties. The organization he founded, the Ambassadors Club, folded in 2004 because of a lack of interest. He is an unknown entity in baseball and African American history. There is no mention of Wimbish at the National Baseball Hall of Fame in Cooperstown, New York. His name is nowhere to be found at Al Lang Field. He is not included in Oxford University Press's authoritative multivolume *African American National Biography* (2008) edited by Harvard Professor Henry Louis Gates, Jr. Most telling is that Wimbish does not have—as of this writing—an entry in Wikipedia, the twenty-first century society's barometer of a historical *Who's Who*.

In fact, aside from the sidewalk marker and his former commercial property, there is no monument, public facility, or street bearing Dr. Wimbish's name in St. Petersburg. Until now, he has never been the subject of a book, a thesis, or an extensive article. Relentless in his quest for racial justice, Dr. Ralph Wimbish risked it all—his livelihood, his house, his personal safety, his family's well being. It is for this that he should be remembered.

# Ralph Wimbish, 1922-1967

Portrait of Ralph Wimbish by Doan Trang.

# Write a Review

If you enjoyed reading *Baseball Under Siege*, take a moment and post a review from where you purchased the book. As an independently published author, reviews are critical to the book's success.

# Author's Note

If you enjoyed reading *Baseball Under Siege,* sign up for my free, quarterly newsletter where you will find out the latest book I'm working on. **Visit www.adamhenig.com to sign-up.** No spam. No selling of emails to a third party. No advertisements. Unsubscribe at any time.

For more information, visit www.adamhenig.com.

# Notes

Notes

Introduction

"Yanks Top Attraction": "Marilyn Monroe Makes Yanks Top Attraction," *Sarasota Hearld-Tribune*, March 28, 1961.

1: The Orange Station Wagon

"You fly down here hot": Alex Haley, "Baseball in a Segregated Town," *SPORT*, July 1961.

"Now you saw that house": Ibid.

"That's it": Ibid.

"I've heard some suites in there": Ibid.

"sauntered or lounged about": Ibid.

"Colored work in there, but that's it!": Ibid.

"Mr. Baseball": "Lang, Mr. Baseball, Dies of Pneumonia," *The Sarasota Herald*, March 28, 1960.

"When you get out of the game today": Haley, "Baseball in a Segregated Town."

"one of the most valuable pieces of property in baseball": Ibid.

"Inside the Cardinals' clubhouse": Ibid.

"lined with hole-in-the-wall restaurants, and dank bars": Ibid.

"not even a decent restaurant for them to eat in": Ibid.

"Block after block": Dorothy Sangster, "The World of Bette Wimbish," *Chatelaine*, September 1963.

2: Becoming Dr. Wimbish

"towering": Sandra W. Rooks, *St. Petersburg, Florida* (Charleston, SC: Arcadia Publishing, 2003), p. 66.

"authoritative voice": Ralph Wimbish Jr. to the author, February 20, 2016.

"constantly cooking and serving": Ellen Babb, "'We Took Leadership Anyway:' Women's Social Activism during the Civil Rights Era in St. Petersburg" in *Making Waves: Female Activists in Twentieth-Century Florida*, Jack E. Davis and Kari Frederickson, eds. (Gainesville: University Press of Florida, 2003), p. 297.

"Wimbish Hotel": Ibid.

"special reputation for midnight kidnappings and mob violence": Claude Andrew Clegg III, *An Original Man: The Life and Times of Elijah Muhammad* (New York: St. Martin's Press, 1997), p. 10.

"two giant fuel tanks that towered over the center": James Harper, "Around the dome, echoes of the past," *St. Petersburg Times*, March 29, 1998.

"the best chicken in town": Ibid.

"No Good Negro:" Ralph Wimbish Jr. to the author, February 20, 2016.

"served as a protective cocoon": Anita S. Cutting, "C. Bette Wimbish and Her Stand for Equality," paper written for Dr. Raymond Aresenault's class, "The United States, 1960-1974," Florida Paper Research Collection Paper, #104, Special Collections and University Archives, Nelson Poynter Memorial Library, University of South Florida, St. Petersburg.

"from the racial attitudes that existed throughout southern society": Ibid.

"morally clean individual, who was honest and upright": Typescript of Chaplain Walter C. Wynn, Tallahassee, Florida, November 7, 1945, in Biographical File of Ralph Melvin Wimbish, Meharry Medical College Library Archives.

"disparaging remarks": Author's interview of Chrystelle Stewart, November 6, 2015.

"I challenge that": Ibid.

"instant superstar status among us premeds": LaSalle D. Leffall Jr., *No Boundaries: A Cancer Surgeon's Odyssey* (Washington, D.C.: Howard University Press, 2005), p. 33.

"one baseball, one baseball bat, and one basketball": Cutting, "C. Bette Wimbish and Her Stand for Equality," p. 4

"red line": Jon L. Wilson, "Shaping the Dream: A Survey of Post-World War II St. Petersburg, 1946-1963," Master's Thesis, p. 88. Special Collections and University Archives, Nelson Poynter Memorial Library, University of South Florida, St. Petersburg, 2009.

"easy he was to talk to": Author's interview of Barbara (Wimbish) Griffin, November 6, 2015.

3: The Ambassadors

"work twice as hard to earn half the income": Hubert Eaton,*Every Man Should Try* (Huntington, WV: Bonaparte Press, 1984), p. 202.

"National Association for the Advancement of *Certain* People": Thomas J. Ward Jr., *Black Physicians in the Jim Crow South*, (Fayetteville, AK: University of Arkansas Press, 2010), p. 285.

"little more than elite social clubs": Ibid.

"medical row": Rosalie Peck and Jon Wilson, *St. Petersburg's Historic 22nd Street South* (Charleston, SC: History Press, 2006), p. 64.

"Gentlemen, let us wake up and do something to help our community": Ibid., p. 16.

"crème de la crème, the elite, the black men": Waveney Ann Moore, "After decades, Ambassador Club set to disband," *St. Petersburg Times*, March 17, 2004.

"first-class": Jon Wilson, "Club played key role in progress of blacks," *St. Petersburg Times*, March 13, 2002.

"queen of the float": Jon Wilson, "Ralph Wimbish and the Ambassador's Club,"*The Weekly Challenger*, September 27, 2012.

"We, as a group of African Americans": Wilson, "Club played key role in progress of blacks."

"Milk Fund Tea": Author's interview of Mordecai Walker, November 5, 2015.

"booming voice:" Ralph Wimbish Jr. to the author, February 20, 2016.

"radical": Ibid.

"What's the point of having separate beaches": Darryl Paulson, "Stay Out, The Water's Fine: Desegregating Municipal Swimming Facilities in St. Petersburg, Florida," *Tampa Bay History* 4 (Fall/Winter 1982), p. 8.

"refused to hear the city's plea": Darryl Paulson, Ibid., p. 10.

"the rumblings of another Little Rock": Ibid., p. 11.

"canvassed the black community": Babb, "'We Took Leadership Anyway,'" p. 298.

"Hamburger Squad": Ibid., p. 299.

"business development": Cutting, "C. Bette Wimbish and Her Stand for Equality."

"Look, all I want to do is sit on the porch and rock my baby": Babb, "'We Took Leadership Anyway,'" p. 300.

"I told Doc Webb's son": "Dr. Fred Alsup was a mover in local civil rights work," [St. Petersburg]*Evening Independent*, February 28, 1985.

"What's wrong with these people?": Ernest Ponder, "A Panoramic Glimpse of Black History in St. Petersburg," The Olive B. McLin Community History Project, 1998, http://faculty.usfsp.edu/jsokolov/mclin/res.4.2.html.

"was scared half to death [when he] peeped in the door": Moore, "After decades, Ambassador Club set to disband."

"Selective Buying": Ponder, "A Panoramic Glimpse of Black History in St. Petersburg."

"Stores that do not treat them [black consumers] with

human dignity": "'No buy' Drive Costs Him $15,000 Daily: Merchants Acts Against NAACP," *The Pittsburgh Courier*, December 31, 1960.

"We are not violent": "100 Negroes Picket Stores, Stage Sit-Ins," *St. Petersburg Times*, December 3, 1960.

"I have waited 30 years in this town": "Dr. Wimbish was a Fighter for Right," [St. Petersburg] *Evening Independent*, December 5, 1967.

"quietly desegregated": Douglas L. Fleming, "Toward Integration: The Course of Race Relations in St. Petersburg, 1868 to 1963," Master's Thesis, p. 56, Special Collections and University Archives, Nelson Poynter Memorial Library, University of South Florida, St. Petersburg, December 1973.,

"most visible": Peyton L. Jones, "Struggle In The Sunshine City: The Movement For Racial Equality In St. Petersburg, Florida, 1955-1968," Master's Thesis, p. 25, Special Collections and University Archives, Nelson Poynter Memorial Library, University of South Florida, St. Petersburg, April 15, 2010.

"because of NAACP's new leadership": Robert W. Saunders to Roy Wilkins, et. al., November 28, 1960, in John H. Bracey, Jr., Sharon Harley, and August Meier, "Papers of the NAACP: Selected Branch Files, 1956-1965, Series A, The South (Bethesda, MD: A microfilm project of the University Publications of America, 1999), Part 27, Reel 3, Frames 671-673.

"full control": Ibid.

"more than 100 people": Ibid.

4: Spring Training in Sunshine City

"unquestioned center of the spring training universe": Charles Fountain, *Under the March Sun: The Story of Spring Training*, (New York: Oxford University Press, 2009), p. 30.

"appeared on 2,500,000 sets in the New York area alone": Wendell Smith, "Sports Beat," *The Pittsburgh Courier*, March 4, 1961.

"meant millions": Fred Lieb, "Al Lang: 'Sunshine Ambassador' for Baseball," *St. Petersburg Times*, March 13, 1975.

"I don't want you sneaking around": David Halberstam, *October 1964* (New York: Random House, 1989), p. 55.

"right attitude":Jules Tygiel, *Baseball's Great Experiment: Jackie Robinson and His Legacy*, (New York: Oxford University Press, 1997), p. 306.

"a certain image": Richard Bak,*Casey Stengal: A Splendid Baseball Life*, (Dallas, TX: Taylor Publishing, 1997), p. 139.

"sweet disposition": Halberstam, *October 1964*, p. 231.

"the perfect player to break the Yankees color line": Ibid., p. 233.

"The camp would break at the end of the day": Peter Golenbock, *Dynasty: The New York Yankees, 1949-1964*, (Chicago: Dover Publications, 2010.), p. 204.

"[We] did what we were supposed to do": Author's interview of Hector Lopez, November 4, 2015.

"Upstairs was where we stayed": Ibid.

5: "We're Not Going to do this Anymore"

"Damn it, we're not going to do this anymore": George Vecsey, *Stan Musial: An American Life*, (New York: Ballantine Books, 2011), p. 243.

"We told the players...we wouldn't be taking them": David K. Rogers, "The spring home of segregation," *St. Petersburg Times*, May 2, 1996.

"The more I thought about it": Haley, "Baseball in a Segregated Town."

"Renting to the major league teams": Jack E. Davis, "Baseball's Reluctant Challenge: Desegregating Major League Spring Training Sites, 1961-1964," *Journal of Sports History*, 19 (Summer 1992), p. 160.

"That was big, easy money in those days": Rogers, "The spring home of segregation."

"I wish I could sign you, too, kid, but I can't": Jerome Holtzman, "Wendell Smith: A Pioneer for Black Athletes," *The Sporting News*, June 22, 1974.

"The time has come for big league owners": Wendell Smith, "Sports Beat: Raps Spring Camp Hotel Bias," *The Pittsburgh Courier*, January 7, 1961.

"Negro Ball Players Want Rights in South": Wendell Smith, "Spring Training Woes: Negro Ball Players Want Rights in South," *Chicago's American*, January 23, 1961.

"like a bunch of vagrants": Ibid.

"The time has come:"Jack Ellison, "Wimbish Declines Usual Assistance: Negro Major Leaguers Face Housing Problems," *St. Petersburg Times*, February 1, 1961.

"Living conditions for the colored players in the Florida

camps": "Spring Camp Segregation: Baseball's Festering Sore," *New York Times*, February 19, 1961.

"It's time management of the clubs takes a hand": "Teams' Help Sought to End Segregation," Ibid., February 1, 1961.

"Wimbish Declines Usual Assistance": Ellison, "Wimbish Declines Usual Assistance."

"Robert": "Teams' Help Sought to End Segregation."

"little change in the practices of past years": "Other Clubs Also Involved: Hope to Have Negro Players Reside in Hotels of Mates," *Milwaukee Journal*, February 2, 1961.

"cancelled reservations because of a ban on Negro guests": Ibid.

"[If] the owners make a united effort to break down segregation": Wendell Smith, "Negro Diamond Stars Tired of Second-Class Citizenship in South," *The Pittsburgh Courier*, February 4, 1961.

"I heard 'nigger' so many times in the outfield": Paul Dickson, *Bill Veeck: Baseball's Greatest Maverick*, (New York: Walker & Company, 2012), p. 129.

"the right time—exactly the right time—to fight it": Smith, "Negro Diamond Stars Tired of Second-Class Citizenship in South."

"If you play like a major leaguer, you should be permitted to live like one": Wendell Smith, "Sports Beat: Campy Speaks out on Diamond Bias in South," *The Pittsburgh Courier*, February 25, 1961.

"It is an outrage": "Sox, Cubs Back Anti-Bias Campaign," *Jet*, February 9, 1961.

"We have never had any trouble and we don't expect any this year": "Yanks Ask 'Under One Roof' Housing in Spring Training," *St. Petersburg Times*, February 2, 1961.

"could put all cities in Florida in danger of losing their spring training clubs": Wayne Shufelt, "Segregation Hassle Won't Affect Braves Stay Here," *The Bradenton* [Florida] *Herald*, February 5, 1961.

"carefully selected homes and...have indicated complete satisfaction": Bob Wolf, "Yanks Seek Integration in Florida; 'Matter No Problem,' Braves Say: Stay in Home at Bradenton," *Milwaukee Journal*, February 2, 1961.

"daily inequities of spring training life": Howard Bryant, *The Last Hero: The Life of Henry Aaron*, (New York: Pantheon Books, 2010), p. 277.

"humiliating reminder": Ibid.

"a tiny, gray-hair [African American] matron": "Spring Camp Segregation: Baseball's Festering Sore."

"sleeping in the hall": Ibid.

"They have nice rooms at Mrs. Gibson's": Shufelt, "Segregation Hassle Won't Affect Braves Stay Here."

"You are going to regret what you are doing": Davis, "Baseball's Reluctant Challenge: Desegregating Major League Spring Training Sites, 1961-1964."

"Mr. Baseball": Frank Caperton, "City's Mr. Baseball is Robbie Robison," *St. Petersburg Times*, April 2, 1966.

"Baseball is the life blood of some of our communities": Haley, "Baseball in a Segregated Town."

"they did not face the same problems": "Other Clubs Also

Involved: Hope to Have Negro Players Reside in Hotels of Mates."

"everyone is welcome at the hotel": Wendell Smith, "Courier Drive Against Baseball Camp Bias Gets Boost: Ricky Backs Move," *The Pittsburgh Courier*, February 4, 1961.

"inform the people in [Arizona] cities": "Sox, Cubs Back Anti-Bias Campaign."

"We're very much in favor of complete integration": Milton Gross, "Seek Owners' Aid in Battle For Spring Training Desegregation," *Chicago's American*, February 1, 1961.

" all Yankee players who wanted stay": "Yanks Ask 'Under One Roof' Housing in Spring Training."

"I want to bring my family to training": Ibid.

"We have always enjoyed having the New York Yankees with us": "Yankees Seek an End to Segregation of Their Players in St. Petersburg," *New York Times*, February 2, 1961.

"Howard, Lopez, and Gonder mean as much to our ball club as any other ball player": Ibid.

"appeared to be the first step toward ending segregation." Ibid.

"We recognize that it is highly desirable for all players to stay together": "Yanks Ask 'Under One Roof' Housing in Spring Training."

"When either the Yankees or the Cardinals": "Cards Already Have Separate Quarters Here," *St. Petersburg Times*, February 3, 1961.

"made more of an effort than any other club": Louis Effrat, "Yanks Offer Reply," *New York Times*, February 3, 1961.

6: Yankees' Departure

"The announcement came as though by accident": "Topping Says Yanks to Move," *St. Petersburg Times*, February 4, 1961.

"there is not a thing we can do about": "Backs *Chicago's American* Campaign: Florida Governor Supports Bias Fight in Spring Camps: Bryant says No Violation of Laws in Integration," *Chicago's American*, February 4, 1961.

"In St. Petersburg, we practice on one field and play on another": "Topping Says Yanks to Move."

"We have nothing against St. Petersburg": "Backs *Chicago's American* Campaign."

"one-year escape clause": Louis Effrat, "Yankees To Abide by Florida Pact," *New York Times*, February 4, 1961.

"We intend to live up to our contract": "Backs *Chicago's American* Campaign."

"Our position in the matter of segregation of players has been made": Effrat, "Yankees To Abide by Florida Pact."

"I repeat that I would like very much to have the whole team under one roof": Ibid.

"took pains to declare that the decision is in no way related to segregation problems": "Topping Says Yanks to Move."

"dead city": Ibid.

"depressing": Ibid.

"Venice of America": "America's Venice: Fort Lauderdale in Florida Making a Bid for Summer Tourists," *New York Times*, May 17, 1959.

"definite plus": Ibid.

"The expressed reason is that they will have Fort Lauderdale to themselves": Alex Haley, "Baseball in a Segregated Town."

"disturbed": Wendell Smith, "Sports Beat," *The Pittsburgh Courier*, March 4, 1961.

"many constructive steps have been taken": Wendell Smith, "*Chicago's American* Spearheads Move: Negro Players Gain Equality Bid," *Chicago's American*, February 6, 1961.

"not rocking the boat": "Arizona and California Camps Free of Segregation Programs," *New York Times*, February 19, 1961.

"we are not spearheading any political movements": Ibid.

"My boys do not mind being subjected to the Jim-Crow laws in the spring": Wendell Smith, "Birdie Tebbets Quit Acting the Part of a 'Baby Chick,'" *The Pittsburgh Courier*, February 18, 1961.

"we would have followed suit": "Spring Camp Segregation: Baseball's Festering Sore."

"It so happens that the sun shines just as bright in the West": Smith, "Sports Beat," March 4, 1961.

"They [city officials who hosted teams during spring training] should seriously contemplate what a baseball exodus": Ibid.

They told me that once you get the first black over there": "Altamese Chapman broke color barrier at hospital," [St. Petersburg] *Evening Independent*, February 28, 1985.

"very nice": Author's interview of Barbara (Wimbish) Griffin, November 6, 2015.

"rookie outfielder who had never swung a bat in the major leagues": Bob Gibson and Lonnie Wheeler. *Stranger to the*

*Game: The Autobiography of Bob Gibson,* (New York: Viking Press, 1994), p. 57.

"I can't stay at the same hotel as the white players": Bill White, *Uppity:My Untold Story About the Games People Play*, (New York: Grand Central Publishing, 2011), p. 73.

"became a national news story": Bill Beck, "Today's Town Meeting Big Story – By Mistake," *St. Petersburg Times*, March 9, 1961.

"convenience to the location of the breakfast only": "Negro Players Get Florida Social Bid," *New York Times*, March 9, 1961.

"Not all ballplayers are eager to get up early in the morning": Beck, "Today's Town Meeting Big Story – By Mistake."

"blanket invitation on the players' bulletin board": Ibid.

"Does this mean me?": Ibid.

"We invited baseball players—not colors": "Negro Players Get Florida Social Bid."

"break down the barriers": Brad Snyder, *A Well-Paid Slave: Curt Flood's Fight for Free Agency in Professional Sports*, (New York: Viking Press, 2006), p. 58.

"Why should I wake up at six in the morning": Arlene Howard with Ralph Wimbish, Jr., *Elston and Me: The Story of the First Black Yankee*, (Columbia, MO: University of Missouri Press, 2001). p. 102.

"If the players are going to pussyfoot over this thing": Bill Nunn, Jr., "Diamond Stars Meet Over Florida Prejudice," *The Pittsburgh Courier*, August 8, 1961.

7: The Fallout

"I am convinced that every white major leaguer views this problem with deep sympathy": "Player Chief Backs Negro Rights Plan," *Chicago's American*, June 19, 1961.

"an issue which baseball cannot dodge": Wendell Smith, "Sports Beat," *The Pittsburgh Courier*, July 1, 1961.

"a brief summary of [each team's] situation with respect to housing all players under one roof": "Historically Significant Lot of Letters to General Managers in 1961 Regarding Negro Housing During Spring Training," Goldin Auctions, Lot #9, accessed on July 1, 2015. . https://goldinauctions.com/Historically_Significant_Lot_of_Letters_to_General-lot5337.aspx

"You folks must be out of your mind": "Letter to Frank Scott from E. J. "Buzzie" Bavasi," August 9, 1961, Goldin Auctions, Lot #9, accessed on July 1, 2015. https://goldinauctions.com/Historically_Significant_Lot_of_Letters_to_General-lot5337.aspx

"cordial": "Letter to Frank Scott and Judge Robert Cannon from Walter O'Malley," August 8, 1961," Goldin Auctions, Lot #9, accessed on July 1, 2015. . https://goldinauctions.com/Historically_Significant_Lot_of_Letters_to_General-lot5337.aspx

"luckiest city in the nation": Joe Kola, "Fort Lauderdale's Stadium Monument to Our Future" *1962 Official New York Yankees Spring Guidebook and Scorecard*, 1962. Spring Training Programs, Magazines, Yearbooks, BA MSS 218, Box 7, Folder 2, National Baseball Hall of Fame Library, Cooperstown, NY.

"It was quite nice": Author interview of Arlene Howard, June 18, 2015.

"making every effort": "Letter from Hank Greenberg to Frank Scott," August 12, 1961, Goldin Auctions, Lot #9, accessed on July 1, 2015. . https://goldinauctions.com/Historically_Significant_Lot_of_Letters_to_General-lot5337.aspx

"flamboyant": Wendell Smith, "$$$ Fight Bias for Owner of White Sox," *The Pittsburgh Courier*, November 25, 1961.

"we have not made any effort to house and feed our negro players": "Letter from Calvin R. Griffin to Frank Scott," August 15, 1961, Goldin Auctions, Lot #9, accessed on July 1, 2015. https://goldinauctions.com/Historically_Significant_Lot_of_Letters_to_General-lot5337.aspx

"people of the area dictate the hotel's policy": "'One Roof' Facility Sought: Phils to Revise Housing," *St. Petersburg Times*, March 10, 1962.

"we can't get accommodations under one roof here we'll try another area": Ibid.

"the one club [in Florida]": "Sports Writer Suggests Detroiters Picket Tigers," *Jet*, May 3, 1962.

"made every effort to house all of our players under one roof in Lakeland": "Letter from a Detroit Tigers representative (unnamed) to Frank Scott," August 19, 1961, Goldin Auctions, Lot #9, accessed on July 1, 2015. https://goldinauctions.com/Historically_Significant_Lot_of_Letters_to_General-lot5337.aspx

"formed a segregation pact with the city": Wendell Smith, "Newest New York Club Set to Carry Bias to Florida," *The Pittsburgh Courier*, April 1, 1961.

"cognizant of the undesirable conditions": "Letter from Bing Devine to Frank Scott," August 17, 1961, Goldin Auctions, Lot #9, accessed on July 1, 2015. https://goldinauctions.com/Historically_Significant_Lot_of_Letters_to_General-lot5337.aspx "a local tourist attraction": Gibson and Wheeler, *Stranger to the Game*, p. 58.

"It was our own little civil rights movement": Ibid., p. 59.

"Baseball's Angry Man": Claire Smith, "Baseball's Angry Man," *New York Times Magazine*, October 13, 1991.

"There are several reasons why I do not like *that* Dome": Steve Baal, "Did We Lose the Giants in the 60s?," *Creative Loafing*, Volume 5, Issue 37, December 16, 1992.

Epilogue

"all references to segregation": Jon Wilson, *The Golden Era in St. Petersburg: Postwar Prosperity in the Sunshine City*, (Charleston, SC: History Press, 2013), p. 135.

"had the power to arrest white people": Wilson, *The Golden Era in St. Petersburg*, p. 131.

"Tonight we're going to integrate this restaurant": White, *Uppity*, p. 79.

"The Devil": Howard, *Elston and Me*, p. 100.

"We can't entirely blame the white community for what is our lot": "Negroes Told They Must Do Their Own Change-making," *St. Petersburg Times*, June 17, 1963.

"Daddy, you need to stop smoking those things": Author's interview of Barbara (Wimbish) Griffin, November 6, 2015.

"zip through law school in just two and half years": Ralph Wimbish Jr., "A warrior, a father, a fighter: Ralph Wimbish waged – and won – many battles at lunch counters, theaters and hotels. His son remembers them, and their cost," *St. Petersburg Times*, November 25, 2007.

"Paralyzed by fear, I couldn't get out of bed": Ibid.

"I'm sorry, I'm sorry. I tried to save him": Ibid.

"the first time [the church] had a full house": Author's interview of Chrystelle Stewart, November 6, 2015.

"a blow to St. Petersburg": Ibid.

"tradition of council members eating lunch together": Kenneth S. Allen, "House race pits underdog against political Goliath," *St. Petersburg Times*, May 16, 1988.

"I can't think of a better way": Raven Joy Shonel, "Honoring C. Bette Wimbish," *The Weekly Challenger*, November 3, 2017.http://theweeklychallenger.com/honoring-c-bette-wimbish/

"no one stepped up": Author's interview of Mordecai Walker, November 5, 2015.

"slowed down": Ibid.

"All this came about because a Negro doctor in St. Petersburg": Jackie Robinson, *Baseball Has Done It*, (Philadelphia: J.B. Lippincott Company, 1964), p. 178.

"had guts": Author's interview of Bill White, June 4, 2015.

"real fighter for civil rights": Ibid.

"key man": Author's interview of Sam Adams, August 13, 2015.

"Dr. Wimbish had a whole lot do": Haley, " Baseball in a Segregated Town."

"There wasn't a white man in Florida—or in baseball, for that matter": Henry Aaron with Lonnie Wheeler, *I Had a Hammer: The Hank Aaron Story*, (New York: HarperCollins Publishers, 1991), p. 153.

# Bibliography

Academic Journals
*Journal of Sports History*
*Tampa Bay History*

Books
Aaron, Henry with Lonnie Wheeler, *I Had a Hammer: The Hank Aaron Story*(New
  York: HarperCollins Publishers, 1991)
Aresenault, Raymond, *St. Petersburg and the Florida Dream, 1888-1950*(Gainesville:
  University Press of Florida, 1996)
Babb, Ellen, "'We Took Leadership Anyway:' Women's Social Activism during the
  Civil Rights Era in St. Petersburg" in *Making Waves: Female Activists in Twentieth-Century Florida*, Jack E. Davis and Kari Frederickson, eds. (Gainesville: University Press of Florida, 2003)
Bak,Richard, *Casey Stengal: A Splendid Baseball Life*(Dallas: Taylor

Publishing, 1997)

Bryant, Howard, *The Last Hero: The Life of Henry Aaron*(New York: Pantheon Books,

2010)

Clegg, Claude Andrew III, *An Original Man: The Life and Times of Elijah Muhammad*

(New York: St. Martin's Press, 1997)

Dickson, Paul, *Bill Veeck: Baseball's Greatest Maverick*, (New York: Walker &

Company, 2012)

Eaton, Hubert, *Every Man Should Try* (Huntington, WV: Bonaparte Press, 1984)

Fountain, Charles, *Under the March Sun: The Story of Spring Training*, (New York:

Oxford University Press, 2009)

Gibson, Bob and Lonnie Wheeler, *Stranger to the Game: The Autobiography of Bob

Gibson*(New York: Viking Press, 1994)

Golenbock, Peter, *Dynasty: The New York Yankees, 1949-1964*(Chicago: Dover

Publications, 2010.)

David Halberstam, *October 1964* (New York: Random House, 1989)

Howard, Arlene with Ralph Wimbish, Jr., *Elston and Me: The Story of the First Black

Yankee*(Columbia, MO: University of Missouri Press, 2001)

Leffall, LaSalle D., Jr., *No Boundaries: A Cancer Surgeon's Odyssey* (Washington, D.C.:

Howard University Press, 2005)

Peck, Rosalie and Jon Wilson, *St. Petersburg's Historic 22nd Street South* (Charleston,

SC: History Press, 2006)

Robinson, Jackie, *Baseball Has Done It*(Philadelphia: J.B. Lippincott Company,

1964)

Rooks, Sandra W., *St. Petersburg, Florida* (Charleston, SC: Arcadia Publishing, 2003)

Snyder, Brad, *A Well-Paid Slave: Curt Flood's Fight for Free Agency in Professional

Sports*(New York: Viking Press, 2006)

Tygiel, Jules, *Baseball's Great Experiment: Jackie Robinson and His Legacy*, (New

York: Oxford University Press, 1997)

Vecsey, George, *Stan Musial: An American Life*(New York: Ballantine Books, 2011)

Ward, Thomas Jr., *Black Physicians in the Jim Crow South*(Fayetteville, AK:

University of Arkansas Press, 2010)

White, Bill, *Uppity:My Untold Story About the Games People Play*(New York:

Grand Central Publishing, 2011)

Wilson, Jon, *The Golden Era in St. Petersburg: Postwar Prosperity in the Sunshine City*

(Charleston, SC: History Press, 2013)

## Magazines and Newspapers

[St. Petersburg]*Evening Independent*
*Chatelaine*[Toronto, Canada]
*Chicago's American*
*Creative Loafing*
*Jet*
*Milwaukee Journal*
*New York Times*
*New York Times Magazine*
*SPORT*
*St. Petersburg Times*
*The Bradenton* [Florida]*Herald*
*The Pittsburgh Courier*
*The Sarasota Herald*
*The Sporting News*
*The Weekly Challenger*

**Manuscript Collections**
Biographical File of Ralph Melvin Wimbish, Meharry Medical College Library Archives.
Papers of the NAACP: Selected Branch Files, 1956-1965 (Bethesda, MD: A microfilm
   project of the University Publications of America, 1999)
   National Baseball Hall of Fame Library, Cooperstown, NY.
   The Olive B. McLin Community History Project
   University of South Florida, St. Petersburg, Special Collections and University Archives, Nelson Poynter Memorial Library

**Interviews**

Sam Adams, August 13, 2015.

Barbara (Wimbish) Griffin, November 6, 2015.

Arlene Howard, June 18, 2015.

Hector Lopez, November 4, 2015.

Jennifer Griffin, November 6, 2015.

Chrystelle Stewart, November 6, 2015.

Paul Stewart, June 17, 2015

Mordecai Walker, November 5, 2015.

Ralph Wimbish, Jr., July 12, 2015, November 6, 2015, and February 20, 2016.

Jon Wilson, July 30, 2015

Bill White, June 4, 2015

# Acknowledgments

When researching and writing about a historical event, an author discovers almost immediately that it is a collective effort.

To begin with, two St. Petersburg, Florida natives — Ralph Wimbish Jr. and Jon Wilson — contributed significantly to the writing of *Baseball Under Siege* (previously titled, *Under One Roof*).

When I contacted Michael Butler of the *Tampa Tribune*, who had written an article about Dr. Wimbish's children, I could not have imagined what would transpire. Responding promptly, Butler put me in touch with Robert Hooker of the *Tribune*, who forwarded my query to Ralph Wimbish Jr. From there, the floodgates opened.

Ralph Jr. provided biographical information regarding his father, and connected me with several of Dr. Wimbish's contemporaries, including retired St. Louis Cardinal first baseman Bill White and Arlene Howard, widow of New York Yankee catcher Elston Howard. Over the course of nine months, Ralph Jr. and I remained in contact via emails and phone calls until we finally met in-person in St. Petersburg. I am profoundly indebted to him for the countless hours he provided in my quest to resurrect the life and times of his father. In addition, Ralph's sister, Barbara (Wimbish) Griffin, shared more about her father than I could have hoped for. Without the cooperation of Ralph and Barbara, I would not have been able to etch a full portrait of their father.

A thirty-year veteran of the *St. Petersburg Times*, Jon Wilson, reporter and author of three books about the Sunshine City, rarely took more than a few hours to respond to many of my questions. Beyond his promptness, Jon was insightful and honest about the turbulent history of the city he knows better than almost anyone. I am also indebted to Jounice Nealy-Brown of the *Times* for putting me in touch with him.

In my search for various documents, primary and secondary, I am most grateful to librarian Jim Schur, who is in charge of the Special Collections & University Archives at the University of South Florida, St. Petersburg. Also, I would like to acknowledge the following research institutions and persons for their support: California State University, East Bay (Carolyn Chun, Jared Mariconi); City of St. Petersburg Historic Preservation Division, Planning and Economic Development Department (Kimberly Hinder, Derek S. Kilborn); Library of Congress (Kia Campbell, Patrick Kerwin); Meharry Medical College Library Archives (Christyne M. Douglas); National Baseball Hall of Fame and Museum (Cassidy Lent); Pinellas County Archives and Library at Heritage Village (Ellen Babb);

St. Petersburg Museum of History (Marta Jones); and *Tampa Bay Times* (Carolyn Edds).

My trip to St. Petersburg would not have been worth my effort if it had not been for the following individuals who answered all of my many questions and in some cases provided access to their institutions: Professor Raymond Aresenault (University of South Florida, St. Petersburg); Peter Belmont (St. Petersburg Preservation); Elihu Brayboy and Carolyn Brayboy (Chief's Creole Cafe); Guy Delaunay (Tampa Bay Rowdies/Al Lang Stadium); and Elaine Normile and Michelle Tyrrell (Vinoy Renaissance St. Petersburg Resort & Golf Club).

I would like to extend my appreciation to the following individuals who provided their time and willingness to speak about Dr. Wimbish: retired journalist and Wimbish friend Sam Adams; Dr. Jennifer Griffin (Dr. Wimbish's granddaughter); Arlene Howard; retired New York Yankee outfielder Hector Lopez (and retired *Tampa Bay Times* journalist Bill Stevens, who introduced me to Mr. Lopez); St. Petersburg residents Wardell Smith and Paul Stewart (and Lyn Jonson of the *Weekly Challenger* for connecting me to Wardell and Paul); Wimbish family friend Chrystelle Stewart (no relation to Paul); former Ambassador Club member Mordecai Walker (and his son Andrew); and, last but not least, Bill White.

I'd also like to acknowledge the following people for their assistance: blogger Jane Friedman; and podcasters Stephen Campbell and Joanna Penn, for helping me—through their respective podcasts—with the business side of being an independently published author; baseball historian Peter Golenbock; George Casteris of Casteris Productions for inviting me to participate in his documentary about the history of spring training; Dr. LaSalle LeFall (Dr. Wimbish's classmate); and Lynette Swain (daughter of Dr. Robert Swain).

*Baseball Under Siege* was independently published. Although I wore several hats throughout the duration of this project, I still relied on a number of professionals in the publishing industry: editors Amy Quale and Savannah Brooks of Wise Ink, who not only did a superb job of editing my manuscript, but raised questions that, in the end, made the book flow smoother and more interesting; Dara Beevas of Wise Ink, who provided direction on my marketing strategy; Liz Mays and Hugh McGuire at Pressbooks; and editor Ashley Clarke for providing the final edits before the manuscript went into production.

My deepest gratitude to my father (and mentor), Professor Emeritus Gerald S. Henig, whose insights and counsel were invaluable. His shared enthusiasm after every nugget of good news I received kept me focused and motivated all the way to the finish line.

To my sisters and their families, aunt, cousins, in-laws, nieces and nephews, co-workers, and friends, I could not have been luckier to have you in my life.

And finally, to my wife, Jennifer, and sons, Jacob and Alex, you are the most precious people to me on this earth.

Sadly, this book was not completed before the passing of my

mother, Lori Henig. There isn't a day that has gone by I haven't thought about her.

# About the Author

Adam Henig is the author of *Watergate's Forgotten Hero: Frank Wills, Night Watchman* (McFarland & Company, Inc., 2021). He is author of two other books, *Alex Haley's Roots: An Author's Odyssey* (2014) and *Baseball Under Siege: The Yankees, the Cardinals, and a Doctor's Battle to Integrate Spring Training* (2016). Adam's writings have appeared in *Time, Detroit Metro Times, Tampa Bay Times, Washington Independent Review of Books, History News Network, San Francisco Book Review,* and the website BlackPast.

For more information, visit www.adamhenig.com.

Made in the USA
Monee, IL
09 January 2024